43
SINCE 1980
Let's grow together
NE능률이
미래를
창조합니다.
건강한 배움의 고객가치를 제공하겠다는 꿈을 실현하기 위해
40년이 넘는 시간 동안 열심히 달려왔습니다.
앞으로도 끊임없는 연구와 노력을 통해
당연한 것을 멈추지 않고
고객, 기업, 직원 모두가 함께 성장하는 NE능률이 되겠습니다.
NE 능률

서문

최근 우리나라 영어 교육의 가장 큰 특징은 실용 영어의 중시와 함께 말하기, 쓰기와 같은 표현 영어를 강조하는 방향으로 변화하고 있다는 점입니다. 근래에 들어 말하기, 쓰기 능력을 평가하려는 시도가 활발해지고 있는 것도 이러한 변화의 일환입니다. 특히 쓰기는 인터넷과 이메일 등 글을 통한 세계와의 접촉이 활발해지는 상황에서 자기 생각을 정확하게 표현하기 위해 반드시 길러야 하는 능력입니다.

쓰기 실력을 향상시키기 위해서는 논리력, 구성력, 표현력 등 여러 가지 능력을 연마해야 합니다. 하지만 우선 영어 문장을 제대로 쓰기 위해 문장의 구조 및 영문법을 이해한 후 이를 바탕으로 충분히 연습해야 합니다. 이에 Writing Builder는 자주 쓰는 문형 및 문법을 익혀 이를 토대로 문장을 써보는 단계적인 학습을 통해 쓰기의 기본기를 탄탄히 쌓을 수 있도록 구성하였습니다. 또한 실생활과 밀접한 상황과 실용문을 통해 영어 문장 쓰기에 친근하게 접근할 수 있도록 하고 풍부한 연습 문제로 영작에 익숙해질 수 있도록 하였습니다.

Writing Builder를 통해 여러분은 영어 문장 쓰는 것에 자신감을 갖고, 나아가 자기 생각을 글로 표현할 수 있게 될 것입니다. Writing Builder가 영어로 글쓰기의 기본을 쌓고자 할 때는 물론, 쓰기 서술형 평가를 준비할 때에도 소중한 디딤돌이 되었으면 합니다.

목차

구성과 특징

영어 문장 쓰기 핵심 Point 정리

문장 쓰기의 기본을 다지는 데 필요한 영어 문장 구조와 문법 사항을 간단명료하게 설명했습니다. 실용적인 예문을 제시하여 한 눈에 보기 쉽게 정리하였습니다.

추가 문법 사항 정리

핵심 Point와 함께 알아 두면 좋은 문법 사항을 정리해 두었습니다.

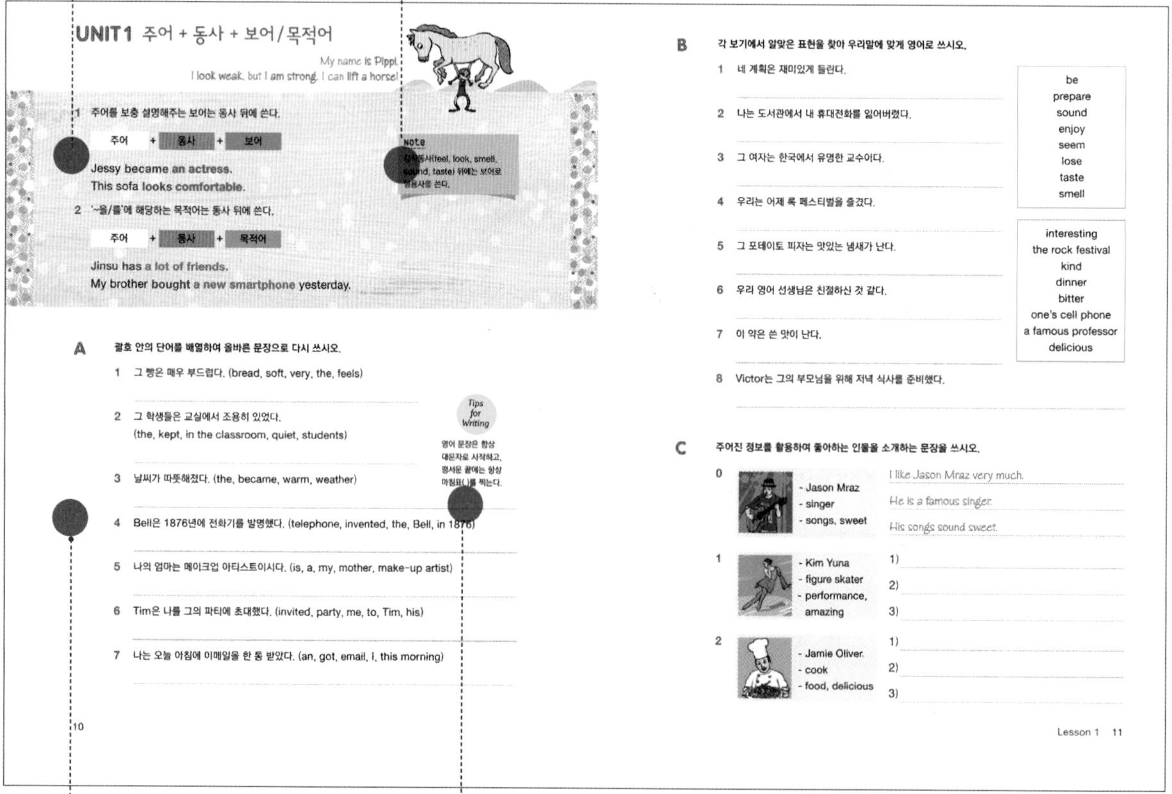

UNIT 1 주어 + 동사 + 보어/목적어

My name is Pippi.
I look weak, but I am strong. I can lift a horse!

1 주어를 보충 설명해주는 보어는 동사 뒤에 쓴다.

주어 + 동사 + 보어

Jessy became an actress.
This sofa looks comfortable.

2 '~을/를'에 해당하는 목적어는 동사 뒤에 쓴다.

주어 + 동사 + 목적어

Jinsu has a lot of friends.
My brother bought a new smartphone yesterday.

Note
감각동사(feel, look, smell, sound, taste) 뒤에는 보어로 형용사를 쓴다.

A 괄호 안의 단어를 배열하여 올바른 문장으로 다시 쓰시오.

1 그 빵은 매우 부드럽다. (bread, soft, very, the, feels)

2 그 학생들은 교실에서 조용히 있었다.
(the, kept, in the classroom, quiet, students)

3 날씨가 따뜻해졌다. (the, became, warm, weather)

4 Bell은 1876년에 전화기를 발명했다. (telephone, invented, the, Bell, in 1876)

5 나의 엄마는 메이크업 아티스트이시다. (is, a, my, mother, make-up artist)

6 Tim은 나를 그의 파티에 초대했다. (invited, party, me, to, Tim, his)

7 나는 오늘 아침에 이메일을 한 통 받았다. (an, got, email, I, this morning)

Tips for Writing
영어 문장은 항상 대문자로 시작하고, 평서문 끝에는 항상 마침표(.)를 찍는다.

10

B 각 보기에서 알맞은 표현을 찾아 우리말에 맞게 영어로 쓰시오.

1 네 계획은 재미있게 들린다.

2 나는 도서관에서 내 휴대전화를 잃어버렸다.

3 그 여자는 한국에서 유명한 교수이다.

4 우리는 어제 록 페스티벌을 즐겼다.

5 그 포테이토 피자는 맛있는 냄새가 난다.

6 우리 영어 선생님은 친절하신 것 같다.

7 이 약은 쓴 맛이 난다.

8 Victor는 그의 부모님을 위해 저녁 식사를 준비했다.

be / prepare / sound / enjoy / seem / lose / taste / smell

interesting / the rock festival / kind / dinner / bitter / one's cell phone / a famous professor / delicious

C 주어진 정보를 활용하여 좋아하는 인물을 소개하는 문장을 쓰시오.

0 - Jason Mraz - singer - songs, sweet
I like Jason Mraz very much.
He is a famous singer.
His songs sound sweet.

1 - Kim Yuna - figure skater - performance, amazing
1)
2)
3)

2 - Jamie Oliver - cook - food, delicious
1)
2)
3)

Lesson 1 11

영어 문장 쓰기의 기본기 다지기

영어 문장 쓰기 실력을 향상시키는 데 필요한 기본적인 기술을 간략하게 설명하였습니다. 이를 통해 좀 더 정확한 문장을 쓸 수 있도록 하였습니다.

다양한 문제 유형을 통한 핵심 Point 연습

다양한 형태의 쓰기 문제를 통해 앞서 학습한 문장 구조 및 문법 사항의 이해도를 점검하고 문장 쓰기의 기초를 마련할 수 있도록 하였습니다.

연습 문제로 핵심 사항 정리

다양하고 심화된 연습 문제로 앞서 학습한 언어 표현과 쓰기 기술을 복습하고, 문장 쓰기에 익숙해질 수 있도록 하였습니다.

영어로 우리말 표현하기

완전한 문장을 직접 써 봄으로써 우리말을 영어로 표현하는 데 자신감을 키울 수 있도록 하였습니다.

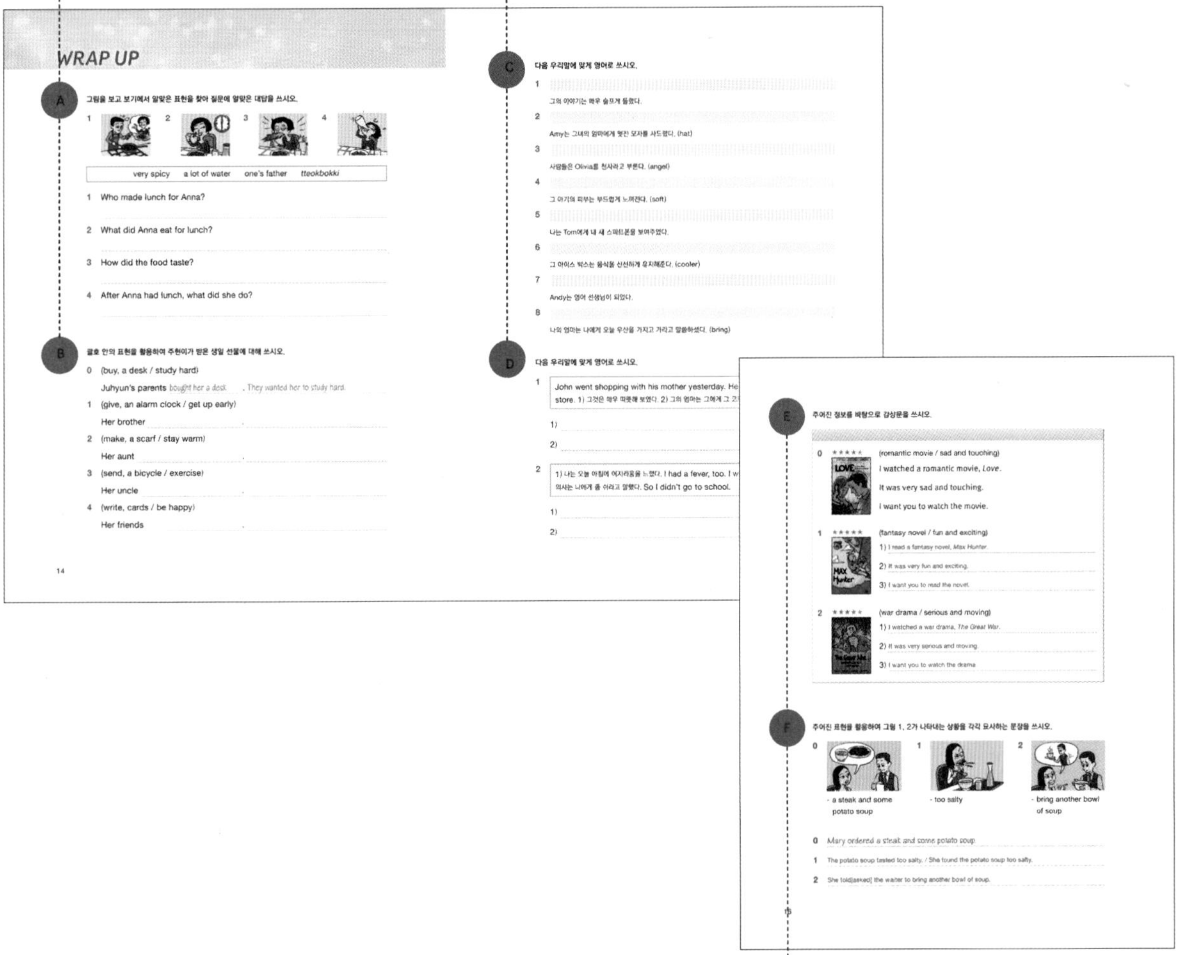

WRAP UP

A 그림을 보고 보기에서 알맞은 표현을 찾아 질문에 알맞은 대답을 쓰시오.

very spicy   a lot of water   one's father   *tteokbokki*

1 Who made lunch for Anna?

2 What did Anna eat for lunch?

3 How did the food taste?

4 After Anna had lunch, what did she do?

B 괄호 안의 표현을 활용하여 주현이가 받은 생일 선물에 대해 쓰시오.

0 (buy, a desk / study hard)

Juhyun's parents bought her a desk. They wanted her to study hard.

1 (give, an alarm clock / get up early)

Her brother .

2 (make, a scarf / stay warm)

Her aunt .

3 (send, a bicycle / exercise)

Her uncle .

4 (write, cards / be happy)

Her friends .

14

C 다음 우리말에 맞게 영어로 쓰시오.

1 그의 이야기는 매우 슬프게 들렸다.

2 Amy는 그녀의 엄마에게 멋진 모자를 사드렸다. (hat)

3 사람들은 Olivia를 천사라고 부른다. (angel)

4 그 아기의 피부는 부드럽게 느껴진다. (soft)

5 나는 Tom에게 내 새 스마트폰을 보여주었다.

6 그 아이스 박스는 음식을 신선하게 유지해준다. (cooler)

7 Andy는 영어 선생님이 되었다.

8 나의 엄마는 나에게 오늘 우산을 가지고 가라고 말씀하셨다. (bring)

D 다음 우리말에 맞게 영어로 쓰시오.

1 John went shopping with his mother yesterday. He store. 1) 그것은 매우 따뜻해 보였다. 2) 그의 엄마는 그에게 그

1)

2)

2 1) 나는 오늘 아침에 어지러움을 느꼈다. I had a fever, too. I w 의사는 나에게 좀 쉬라고 말했다. So I didn't go to school.

1)

2)

E 주어진 정보를 바탕으로 감상문을 쓰시오.

0 ★★★★★ (romantic movie / sad and touching)

I watched a romantic movie, *Love*.

It was very sad and touching.

I want you to watch the movie.

1 ★★★★★ (fantasy novel / fun and exciting)

1) I read a fantasy novel, *Max Hunter*.

2) It was very fun and exciting.

3) I want you to read the novel.

2 ★★★★★ (war drama / serious and moving)

1) I watched a war drama, *The Great War*.

2) It was very serious and moving.

3) I want you to watch the drama.

F 주어진 표현을 활용하여 그림 1, 2가 나타내는 상황을 각각 묘사하는 문장을 쓰시오.

0 - a steak and some potato soup

1 - too salty

2 - bring another bowl of soup

0 Mary ordered a steak and some potato soup

1 The potato soup tasted too salty. / She found the potato soup too salty.

2 She told[asked] the waiter to bring another bowl of soup.

15

실용문과 서술형 평가 문제로 응용력 기르기

앞서 학습한 표현을 활용하여 일기, 이메일, 광고문 등의 실용문을 완성해 보고, 서술형 평가와 유사한 문제를 풀어봄으로써 응용력을 기를 수 있도록 하였습니다.

필수 문장 표현 익히기

사용 빈도가 높은 문장 패턴을 선별하여
실생활에서 자주 쓰이는 문장 표현에 익숙해질 수
있도록 하였습니다.

Useful Patterns **for Writing 1**

* be curious about ~: ~에 대해 궁금해하다
I am curious about your hobby.

* be aware of ~: ~을 알고 있다
I am aware of his opinion.

1 그 아이들은 그 작은 동물에 대해 궁금해했다. (kid)

2 Rosa는 그녀의 문제에 대해 알고 있었다.

3 나는 하늘에 있는 별들이 궁금하다.

4 David는 내 나쁜 습관들을 알고 있다.

5 그는 우리의 새로운 계획에 대해 궁금해했다.

6 우리는 우리의 상황을 알고 있다. (situation)

7 사람들은 그의 새 책에 대해 궁금해한다.

8 Jane은 그 중요한 사실을 알고 있다. (fact)

9 Sally는 그 잘생긴 배우가 궁금했었다.

10 그들은 학교 규칙들에 대해 알고 있다. (rule)

109

어휘 복습하기

Lesson별 중요 어휘를 복습하고 암기할 수
있도록 하였습니다.

LESSON 1

actress 여배우
comfortable 편안한
soft 부드러운
classroom 교실
invent 발명하다
—
invite 초대하다
famous 유명한
professor 교수
festival 축제
delicious 맛있는
—
seem ~인 것 같다
medicine 약
bitter 쓴
prepare 준비하다
sweet 달콤한
—
performance 공연, 연주회
secret 비밀
lawyer 변호사
expect 기대하다
athlete 운동 선수
—
text message 문자 메시지
useful 유용한
director 감독
advise 충고하다
report card 성적표
—
angry 화난
nervous 불안한, 초조한
spicy 매운
hard 열심히
exercise 운동하다
—
angel 천사
cooler 아이스박스
fresh 신선한
bring 가져가다
dizzy 어지러운
—
rest 휴식
touching 감동적인
fun 재미있는
serious 심각한
moving 가슴을 뭉클하게 하는
—
bowl 그릇
salty 짠, 짭짤한

LESSON 2

roof 지붕
trouble 문제
touch 만지다
shake 흔들리다
P.E. 체육
—
magic 마술
bark (개 등이) 짖다
cross 건너다
rise 오르다, 올라가다
clothes 옷
—
essay 에세이
earring 귀걸이
slim 날씬한
hang 매달다
subway 지하철
—
hospital 병원
plant 식물
hose 호스
stay 머무르다
on time 정각에
—
check 확인하다
sunset 해질녘, 일몰
take a shower 샤워를 하다
arrive 도착하다
cartoon 만화
—
character 등장인물
shoulder 어깨
scream 비명을 지르다
haunted house 유령의 집
parade 퍼레이드, 가두 행진
—
gym 체육관
coach 코치
pass (공을) 패스하다
credit card 신용카드
make fun of ~을 놀리다
—
ship 배, 선박
enter 들어가다
fight 싸우다
on foot 걸어서, 도보로
ride 타다
—
cherry blossoms 벚꽃

122

SECTION 1

SENTENCE STRUCTURE

LESSON 1

문장의 형식

UNIT 1 주어 + 동사 + 보어 / 목적어
UNIT 2 주어 + 동사 + 간접목적어 + 직접목적어 / 주어 + 동사 + 목적어 + 목적보어

weak	delicious	athlete	angel
actress	seem	text message	cooler
comfortable	medicine	useful	fresh
soft	bitter	director	bring
classroom	prepare	advise	dizzy
invent	sweet	report card	rest
invite	performance	nervous	touching
famous	secret	spicy	fun
professor	lawyer	hard	serious
festival	expect	exercise	moving

UNIT 1 주어 + 동사 + 보어/목적어

My name is Pippi.
I look weak, but I am strong. I can lift a horse!

1 주어를 보충 설명해주는 보어는 동사 뒤에 쓴다.

주어	+	동사	+	보어

Jessy **became** an actress.
This sofa **looks** comfortable.

Note
감각동사(feel, look, smell, sound, taste) 뒤에는 보어로 형용사를 쓴다.

2 '~을/를'에 해당하는 목적어는 동사 뒤에 쓴다.

주어	+	동사	+	목적어

Jinsu **has** a lot of friends.
My brother **bought** a new smartphone yesterday.

A 괄호 안의 단어를 배열하여 올바른 문장으로 다시 쓰시오.

1 그 빵은 매우 부드럽다. (bread, soft, very, the, feels)

....

2 그 학생들은 교실에서 조용히 있었다.
(the, kept, in the classroom, quiet, students)

....

Tips for Writing
영어 문장은 항상 대문자로 시작하고, 평서문 끝에는 항상 마침표(.)를 찍는다.

3 날씨가 따뜻해졌다. (the, became, warm, weather)

....

4 Bell은 1876년에 전화기를 발명했다. (telephone, invented, the, Bell, in 1876)

....

5 나의 엄마는 메이크업 아티스트이시다. (is, a, my, mother, make-up artist)

....

6 Tim은 나를 그의 파티에 초대했다. (invited, party, me, to, Tim, his)

....

7 나는 오늘 아침에 이메일을 한 통 받았다. (an, got, email, I, this morning)

....

B

각 보기에서 알맞은 표현을 찾아 우리말에 맞게 영어로 쓰시오.

보기 1
be
prepare
sound
enjoy
seem
lose
taste
smell

보기 2
interesting
the rock festival
kind
dinner
bitter
one's cell phone
a famous professor
delicious

1 네 계획은 재미있게 들린다.

....

2 나는 도서관에서 내 휴대전화를 잃어버렸다.

....

3 그 여자는 한국에서 유명한 교수이다.

....

4 우리는 어제 록 페스티벌을 즐겼다.

....

5 그 포테이토 피자는 맛있는 냄새가 난다.

....

6 우리 영어 선생님은 친절하신 것 같다.

....

7 이 약은 쓴 맛이 난다.

....

8 Victor는 그의 부모님을 위해 저녁 식사를 준비했다.

....

C

주어진 정보를 활용하여 좋아하는 인물을 소개하는 문장을 쓰시오.

0

- Jason Mraz
- singer
- songs, sweet

I like Jason Mraz very much.

He is a famous singer.

His songs sound sweet.

1

- Kim Yuna
- figure skater
- performance, amazing

1) ....

2) ....

3) ....

2

- Jamie Oliver
- cook
- food, delicious

1) ....

2) ....

3) ....

UNIT 2 주어 + 동사 + 간접목적어 + 직접목적어 / 주어 + 동사 + 목적어 + 목적보어

A school **makes me bored.**
Don't **tell me to go to school.**

1 '~에게 …을 (-해)주다'를 표현할 때는, 동사 뒤에 간접목적어(~에게)와 직접목적어(…을)를 차례로 쓴다.

주어	+	수여동사	+	간접목적어	+	직접목적어

Our teacher **gave us a lot of homework.**
Mike **told me his secret.**

2 목적어를 보충 설명해주는 목적보어는 목적어 뒤에 쓴다.

주어	+	동사	+	목적어	+	목적보어

We **call our dog Eddie.** I **found the book sad.**
My parents **want me to be a lawyer.**

Note

1 수여동사
give, buy, teach, send, show, lend, make, bring, ask, tell, write 등

2 목적보어로 to부정사(구)를 취하는 동사
want, advise, ask, tell, expect 등

A 괄호 안의 단어를 배열하여 올바른 문장으로 다시 쓰시오.

1 Emma는 나에게 피자를 좀 만들어주었다. (pizza, Emma, made, some, me)

---

2 우리는 그 선수가 금메달을 따길 기대했다.
(expected, the, we, win, to, a, athlete, gold medal)

---

3 그들은 그들의 아기를 Sam이라고 이름 지었다. (their, named, baby, they, Sam)

---

4 Ron이 나에게 문자메시지를 보냈다.(me, text message, Ron, sent, a)

---

5 나는 그 웹사이트가 유용하다는 것을 알았다. (found, I, website, the, useful)

---

6 Dan은 내가 그 파티에 오기를 원했다. (wanted, to the party, me, Dan, come, to)

B

각 보기에서 알맞은 표현을 찾아 우리말에 맞게 영어로 쓰시오.

keep teach show advise find lend make tell

home open a famous director difficult English a lot of books one's picture one's notebook

1 나는 내 친구들에게 내 사진을 보여주었다.

....

2 그 영화는 그를 유명한 감독으로 만들었다.

....

3 Ms. Baker는 작년에 우리에게 영어를 가르쳐주셨다.

....

4 나의 선생님은 내게 많은 책을 읽으라고 충고하셨다.

....

5 Harry는 그 시험이 어렵다는 것을 알았다.

....

6 Eva는 어제 나에게 그녀의 공책을 빌려주었다.

....

7 나의 부모님께서 나에게 집에 일찍 오라고 말씀하셨다.

....

8 Kevin은 창문을 열어 두었다.

....

C

괄호 안의 표현을 활용하여 다음과 같이 문장을 쓰시오.

0 

(show, one's report card / angry)

Jina *showed her father her report card* .

It made him angry.

1 

(send, flowers / happy)

1) John ....

2) ....

2 

(ask, a difficult question / nervous)

1) The teacher ....

2) ....

WRAP UP

A 그림을 보고 보기에서 알맞은 표현을 찾아 질문에 알맞은 대답을 쓰시오.

1 

2 

3 

4 

very spicy	a lot of water	one's father	*tteokbokki*

1 Who made lunch for Anna?

____

2 What did Anna eat for lunch?

____

3 How did the food taste?

____

4 After Anna had lunch, what did she do?

____

B 괄호 안의 표현을 활용하여 주현이가 받은 생일 선물에 대해 쓰시오.

0 (buy, a desk / study hard)

Juhyun's parents bought her a desk. They wanted her to study hard.

1 (give, an alarm clock / get up early)

Her brother ______________. ______________

2 (make, a scarf / stay warm)

Her aunt ______________. ______________

3 (send, a bicycle / exercise)

Her uncle ______________. ______________

4 (write, cards / be happy)

Her friends ______________. ______________

C 다음 우리말에 맞게 영어로 쓰시오.

1

그의 이야기는 매우 슬프게 들렸다.

2

Amy는 그녀의 엄마에게 멋진 모자를 사드렸다. (hat)

3

사람들은 Olivia를 천사라고 부른다. (angel)

4

그 아기의 피부는 부드럽게 느껴진다. (soft)

5

나는 Tom에게 내 새 스마트폰을 보여주었다.

6

그 아이스 박스는 음식을 신선하게 유지해준다. (cooler)

7

Andy는 영어 선생님이 되었다.

8

나의 엄마는 나에게 오늘 우산을 가지고 가라고 말씀하셨다. (bring)

D 다음 우리말에 맞게 영어로 쓰시오.

1

John went shopping with his mother yesterday. He found a nice coat at a store. 1) 그것은 매우 따뜻해 보였다. 2) 그의 엄마는 그에게 그 코트를 사주셨다.

1) ______

2) ______

2

1) 나는 오늘 아침에 어지러움을 느꼈다. I had a fever, too. I went to the doctor. 2) 그 의사는 나에게 좀 쉬라고 말했다. So I didn't go to school.

1) ______ (dizzy)

2) ______ (get some rest)

E 주어진 정보를 바탕으로 감상문을 쓰시오.

0 ★★★★★

(romantic movie / sad and touching)

I watched a romantic movie, *Love*.

It was very sad and touching.

I want you to watch the movie.

1 ★★★★★

(fantasy novel / fun and exciting)

1) ....

2) ....

3) ....

2 ★★★★★

(war drama / serious and moving)

1) ....

2) ....

3) ....

F 주어진 표현을 활용하여 그림 1, 2가 나타내는 상황을 각각 묘사하는 문장을 쓰시오.

0

- a steak and some potato soup

1

- too salty

2

- bring another bowl of soup

0 Mary ordered a steak and some potato soup.

1 ....

2 ....

LESSON 2

문장 형식의 심화

UNIT 1 지각동사/사역동사 + 목적어 + 동사원형
UNIT 2 여러 개의 부사(구) 쓰기

roof	earring	take a shower	ride
trouble	slim	arrive	haunted house
touch	hang	airport	pass
shake	subway	bus stop	credit card
P.E. teacher	hospital	draw	make fun of
bark	plant	ship	fight
cross	hose	cartoon	enjoy
rise	stay	character	playground
clothes	check	shoulder	put out
essay	sunset	scream	bring

UNIT 1 지각동사/사역동사 + 목적어 + 동사원형

People **saw Pippi play** on the roof.
Police officers don't **let her make** trouble.

★ 지각동사와 사역동사는 목적보어로 동사원형을 쓴다.

주어	+	지각 / 사역동사	+	목적어	+	동사원형

I **saw a UFO fly** in the sky.
He **felt someone touch** his back.

Her joke **made us laugh**.
My parents **let me have** a dog.

Note

1 **지각동사**: 감각기관을 통해 느끼는 것을 표현하는 동사
see, watch, hear, feel 등

2 **사역동사**: 문장의 주체가 다른 사람 또는 사물이 어떤 행위를 하도록 하는 것을 표현하는 동사
make, have, let

A 괄호 안의 단어를 배열하여 올바른 문장으로 다시 쓰시오.

1 나의 오빠는 내가 라면을 끓이도록 시켰다. (my, brother, cook, ramen, made, me)

2 나는 Joe가 플루트를 연주하는 것을 들었다. (I, play, flute, heard, the, Joe)

3 사람들은 그 건물이 흔들리는 것을 느꼈다. (felt, the, people, shake, building)

4 우리 체육 선생님은 우리를 빨리 달리도록 시키셨다.
(our, run, P.E. teacher, had, us, fast)

5 우리는 그 남자가 마술하는 것을 보았다. (the, do, watched, we, man, magic)

6 나는 매일 밤 그 개가 짖는 것을 듣는다. (hear, bark, every night, dog, I, the)

7 나의 선생님께서 내가 집에 일찍 가는 것을 허락하셨다.
(let, go, early, my, home, me, teacher)

8 나는 Ted가 그 길을 건너는 것을 보았다. (Ted, the, street, cross, saw, I)

B 보기에서 알맞은 표현을 찾아 우리말에 맞게 영어로 쓰시오.

talk on the phone clean one's room rise over the sea read one's essay learn taekwondo wear one's clothes touch one's bag

1 우리는 바다 위로 태양이 떠오르는 것을 보았다.

2 나의 엄마는 내가 나의 방을 청소하게 시키신다.

3 나는 누군가가 내 가방을 만지는 것을 느꼈다.

4 나의 언니는 내가 그녀의 옷을 입는 것을 허락하지 않는다.

5 Amy는 그녀의 아빠가 전화로 말씀하시는 것을 들었다.

6 나의 부모님께서는 나에게 태권도를 배우게 하셨다.

7 Jim은 어제 내가 그의 에세이를 읽는 것을 허락했다.

C 그림을 보고 괄호 안의 표현을 활용하여 친구들의 복장에 대한 문장을 쓰시오.

0 

- Jenny

(earrings / pretty)

I saw Jenny wear earrings.

They made her look prettier.

1 

- Jungi

(white jeans / slim)

1)

2)

2 

- Misun

(high heels / tall)

1)

2)

UNIT 2 여러 개의 부사(구) 쓰기

I can hang from the chandelier by my legs all day.

★ 여러 개의 부사(구)를 쓸 때는 보통 〈장소 + 방법 · 수단 + 시간〉 순서로 쓴다.

I go **to school by subway every morning.**
Nick was **in the hospital for a month.**
Mark is watering the plants **in the garden with a hose.**

Note

1 **장소의 전치사**
in(~안에), at(~에), on(~위에), under(~아래에), by(~옆에), next to(~옆에)

2 **방법 · 수단의 전치사**
by(~로), with(~을 가지고)

3 **시간의 전치사**
at(구체적인 시각), in(오전, 오후, 월, 계절, 연도), on(날짜, 요일, 특정한 날)

A **괄호 안의 단어를 배열하여 올바른 문장으로 다시 쓰시오.**

1 Emily는 2주 동안 영국에 머물렀다. (England, two weeks, stayed, in, for, Emily)

2 Joe는 매일 정시에 학교에 온다. (Joe, to, on, comes, time, every day, school)

3 나는 매일 아침 나의 스마트폰으로 날씨를 확인한다.
(check, every morning, I, my, the, smartphone, weather, with)

4 너는 해가 지기 전에 집에 와야 한다. (should, you, before, come, sunset, home)

5 나는 어제 TV에서 그 뉴스를 봤다. (on, yesterday, the, TV, news, I, watched)

6 나의 아빠는 금요일에 자전거로 일하러 가신다.
(by, Fridays, work, on, to, my, goes, father, bicycle)

7 Lucy는 오후에 집에 있었다. (was, in, at, Lucy, the, afternoon, home)

8 Jason은 그의 친구들을 공원에서 5시에 만났다.
(in, his, Jason, five, the, park, met, at, friends)

B 각 보기에서 알맞은 표현을 찾아 우리말에 맞게 영어로 쓰시오.

the restaurant
a pencil
Busan
the library
the bus stop
church
cold water
the airport

yesterday
the morning
three hours
weekends
six thirty
thirty minutes
last year
Sundays

1 나는 작년에 부산에서 살았다.

____

2 Dan은 일요일마다 버스로 교회를 간다.

____

3 Sarah는 세 시간 동안 도서관에서 책 한 권을 읽었다.

____

4 나는 아침에 찬물로 샤워를 했다.

____

5 그는 공항에 6시 30분에 도착할 것이다.

____

6 나는 30분 동안 버스정류장에서 기다렸다.

____

7 Eva는 주말에 레스토랑에서 일한다.

____

8 그는 어제 그 그림을 연필로 그렸다.

____

C 주어진 정보를 활용하여 여행 일정에 대한 문장을 쓰시오.

0
- Gwangju
- plane, May 6th
- a week

I will go to Gwangju by plane on May 6th.

I will stay in Gwangju for a week.

1
- Jeju
- ship, October 16th
- three days

1) _______________

2) _______________

2
- Gyeongju
- KTX, August 3rd
- the weekend

1) _______________

2) _______________

WRAP UP

A 다음은 놀이공원의 모습이다. 그림을 보고 각 보기에서 알맞은 표현을 찾아 질문에 알맞은 대답을 쓰시오.

0 

1 

2 

3 

cartoon characters	someone	people

walk down	touch one's shoulder	scream

0 What did Inseon see at the ticket box?

She saw people wait in line at the ticket box.

1 What did Inseon hear near the Viking ride?

2 What did Inseon feel in the haunted house?

3 What did Inseon watch on the street?

B 민지의 다이어리를 보고 괄호 안의 단어를 활용하여 민지의 주말 일과에 대해서 쓰시오.

0 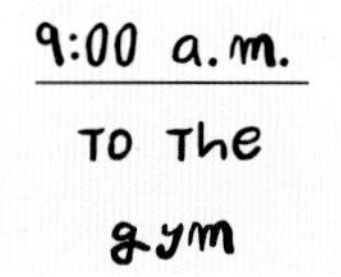

1 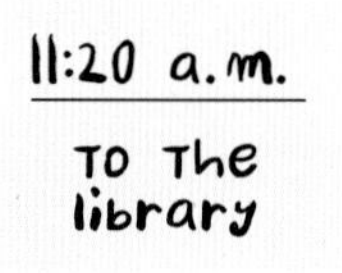

2 

3 

0 Minji goes to the gym on foot at 9:00 a.m. (foot)

1 (subway)

2 (bus)

3 (foot)

C 다음 우리말에 맞게 영어로 쓰시오.

1

Chris는 누군가가 그의 이름을 부르는 것을 들었다. (someone)

2

Linda는 2년 동안 파리에서 불어를 공부했다. (French)

3

그 감독은 그 선수들이 공을 패스하는 것을 지켜보았다. (coach)

4

Mr. Pitt은 내가 매일 피아노를 연습하도록 시키신다. (make, practice)

5

나는 지난 일요일에 이 치마를 내 신용카드로 샀다. (credit card)

6

나는 Sarah가 그녀의 친구들과 함께 점심을 먹는 것을 보았다.

7

David는 이번 토요일에 배로 일본에 갈 것이다. (ship)

8

나의 오빠는 어젯밤에 내가 그의 태블릿 PC를 사용하는 것을 허락했다. (tablet PC)

D 다음 우리말에 맞게 영어로 쓰시오.

1

> Tom made fun of me today. I was angry and I fought with him. Suddenly, my teacher entered the classroom. 1) 그녀는 우리가 싸우는 것을 봤다. 2) 그녀는 우리가 교실을 청소하도록 시켰다.

1) ....

2) .... (make)

2

> 1) 나는 어제 KTX를 타고 부산에 갔다. Haeundae beach was so beautiful. 2) 우리는 오후에 바다에서 수영을 했다. It was very fun.

1) ....

2) ....

E 주어진 정보를 바탕으로 일기를 쓰시오.

0

- the Han River
- bus
- ride the swan boats

I went to the Han River today.
I went there by bus.
I saw many people ride the swan boats.

1

- Namsan
- foot
- ride cable cars

1) ______________________
2) ______________________
3) ______________________

2

- Yeouido
- subway
- enjoy cherry blossoms

1) ______________________
2) ______________________
3) ______________________

F 다음 그림을 보고 보기의 단어와 괄호 안의 표현을 활용하여 그림이 나타내는 상황을 묘사한 문장을 쓰시오.

bring a ball draw a line put out bases

There are some students on the playground.

1 The teacher made ______________________. (two girls)

2 ______________________ (a tall boy)

3 ______________________ (a girl)

LESSON 3

문장의 확장 I

UNIT 1 시간을 나타내는 접속사
UNIT 2 이유 · 결과 · 조건을 나타내는 접속사
UNIT 3 목적절의 접속사로 쓰인 that

right away	lose	tired	experience
turn off	wallet	tell a lie	information
heater	imagine	grade	enjoyment
go out	win	amusement	expensive
wipe	first prize	turn on	be over
prepare	smart	attend	seem
warm up	class	meeting	save
fall	review	catch a cold	advantage
asleep	material	right	practical
take care of	take a note	math	skip

UNIT 1 시간을 나타내는 접속사

After I have meals, I clean them up right away.
It is easy.

★ 시간을 나타내는 접속사 when(~할 때), while(~하는 동안), before(~전에), after(~후에)를 써서 절과 절을 연결할 수 있다.

I will call you **when** I arrive at the station.
While you were sleeping, Maria called you.
Wash your hands **before** you cook.
After I exercise, I feel good.

Note
시간의 부사절에서 현재시제가 미래를 대신한다.

A

다음 두 문장을 괄호 안의 단어를 이용하여 한 문장으로 쓰시오.

Tips for Writing
부사절이 주절 앞에 오면 부사절 다음에 쉼표(,)를 쓴다. 부사절이 주절 뒤에 오면 쓰지 않는다.

1 Turn off the heater. You go out. (before)

2 You cross the street. You must be careful. (when)

3 Dohyung wiped the table. His mother was preparing dinner. (while)

4 You swim. You should warm up. (before)

5 Cindy lived in Sydney. She was ten years old. (when)

6 Mike was watching the baseball game. He fell asleep. (while)

7 I can play a computer game. I finish my homework. (after)

8 I am at my uncle's house. Take care of my dog. (while)

9 I traveled around England. The weather was beautiful. (when)

B 보기에서 알맞은 표현을 찾아 우리말에 맞게 영어로 쓰시오. (단, 부사절은 앞에 쓰시오.)

go out travel in Europe come arrive at graduate

1 비가 오기 전에 우리는 집에 도착했다.

2 Tom은 유럽을 여행하는 동안 많은 친구들을 사귀었다.

3 나는 졸업한 후에 작가가 되길 원한다.

4 Allie는 집에 왔을 때 피곤해 보였다.

5 당신이 밖에 나가기 전에 창문을 닫아 주세요.

UNIT 2 이유 · 결과 · 조건을 나타내는 접속사

If you like to skate, your house will be clean.

1 '~이기 때문에'라는 의미로 이유를 나타낼 때 because를, '그래서'라는 의미로 결과를 나타낼 때 so를 쓴다.
Junwoo was angry **because** I told him a lie.
I worked all day, **so** I am very tired.

2 '~한다면, ~라면'이라는 의미로 조건을 나타낼 때 if를 쓰며, '만약 ~하지 않으면'이라는 의미로는 unless를 쓴다.
If you need a camera, I can lend you mine.
Unless you get up early, you will miss the school bus.

Note
조건의 부사절에서 현재시제가 미래를 대신한다.

A 다음 두 문장을 괄호 안의 단어를 이용하여 한 문장으로 쓰시오.

1 Peter went to bed early. He felt sick. (because)

2 You are hungry. You can eat lunch now. (if)

3 There was a traffic jam. I took the subway. (so)

4 You study hard. You won't get good grades. (unless)

5 It was too hot. I couldn't sleep well. (because)

6 I will go to the amusement park. It is sunny tomorrow. (if)

Tips for Writing

so로 문장과 문장을 연결할 때에는 so 앞에 쉼표(,)를 사용하여 그 의미를 더 분명히 할 수 있다.

B **보기에서 알맞은 표현을 찾아 우리말에 맞게 영어로 쓰시오. (단, 부사절은 앞에 쓰시오.)**

catch a cold
turn on the heater
have breakfast
attend the meeting
come to the party

1 나는 너무 추워서 히터를 켰다.

2 Jay는 아팠기 때문에 그는 미팅에 참석하지 않았다.

3 네가 Harry를 본다면, 그에게 파티에 오라고 말해줘.

4 나는 늦게 일어났기 때문에 아침 식사를 하지 않았다.

5 네가 따뜻한 코트를 입지 않으면, 너는 감기에 걸릴 것이다.

UNIT 3 목적절의 접속사로 쓰인 that

*I think **that** I cannot draw this big horse on small paper.*

★ 절을 동사의 목적어로 쓸 때에는 그 절 앞에 접속사 that을 쓴다.

Lily believes **that** she is right.

Susan knew **that** Suhyun lied to her.

I think **that** the exam was difficult.

A **보기에서 알맞은 표현을 찾아 우리말에 맞게 영어로 쓰시오.**

be the smartest
love me
win first prize
lose one's wallet
be on the moon
travel to China
be difficult

1 많은 학생들이 수학은 어렵다고 생각한다.

2 나는 나의 부모님이 나를 아주 많이 사랑하시는 것을 안다.

3 Dan은 지난주에 그의 지갑을 잃어버렸다고 말했다.

4 우리가 달에 있다고 상상해보자.

5 우리는 우리 팀이 일등상을 탈 것이라고 믿는다.

6 나는 Jessica가 우리 반에서 가장 똑똑하다고 생각한다.

7 Jim은 이번 여름에 중국으로 여행하기를 희망한다.

B **그림을 보고 괄호 안의 표현을 활용하여 가족들의 문제점에 대해 쓰시오.**

0 

(father, lie on the sofa)

I think that my father lies on the sofa too much.

I hope that he lies[will lie] on the sofa less.

1 

(mother, shop online)

1)

2)

2 

(brother, play games)

1)

2)

WRAP UP

A

괄호 안의 단어와 각 보기의 표현을 활용하여 좋은 성적을 얻을 수 있는 방법에 대해 쓰시오.

make a study plan review the class materials take notes	you are in class the class finishes you study

0 *Don't listen to music while you are studying.* (while)

1 ______________________ (before)

2 ______________________ (after)

3 ______________________ (when)

B

그림을 보고 보기에서 알맞은 표현을 찾아 그림이 표현하는 바를 쓰시오.

0 

- books

1 

- traveling

2 

- the Internet

3 

- friends

useful information	a lot of enjoyment	a good rest

0 *I think that books give us many experiences.*

1 ______________________

2 ______________________

3 ______________________

C 다음 우리말에 맞게 영어로 쓰시오. (단, 부사절은 앞에 쓰시오.)

1

인도인들은 먹을 때 그들의 손들을 사용한다. (Indian)

2

나는 내 휴대전화를 잃어버려서 네게 전화할 수 없었다.

3

그 모자가 너무 비쌌기 때문에 Joan은 그것을 사지 않았다.

4

그 기차가 떠난 후에 나는 역에 도착했다.

5

당신이 도서관 카드를 가지고 있지 않다면 책들을 빌릴 수 없습니다. (library card)

6

Ron은 기다리고 있던 동안 잡지를 읽었다. (magazine)

7

나는 David가 좋은 축구 선수가 될 것이라고 믿는다. (become)

D 다음 우리말에 맞게 영어로 쓰시오.

1

1) Katie는 아팠기 때문에 오늘 학교에 오지 않았다. I was worried, so I called her. 2) 내가 그녀에게 전화했을 때 그녀는 자고 있었다. I hope that she will get better soon.

1) ______________________________

2) ______________________________

2

Tomorrow is Parents' Day. 1) 나는 학교가 끝난 후에 백화점에 갈 것이다. I will buy a tie for my father and earrings for my mother. 2) 나는 그들이 내 선물들을 좋아하길 바란다.

1) ______________________________ (be over)

2) ______________________________

E

주어진 정보를 바탕으로 구입한 물건의 후기를 쓰시오.

0		- color, nice / uncomfortable, wear I think that the color is nice. But they seem uncomfortable when I wear them.
1	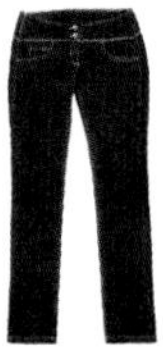	- design, pretty / tight, wear 1) ____________ 2) ____________
2		- size, small / heavy, carry 1) ____________ 2) ____________

F

보기에서 온라인 강의의 장점과 단점에 해당하는 표현을 한 개씩 골라 그 장점과 단점에 대한 문장을 쓰시오.

Advantages	**Disadvantages**
- save money / useful	- skip class easily / not useful
- take classes again later / helpful	- not focus on classes / not helpful

Advantages

0 Online classes are good because students can save time.

I think that they are practical.

1 ____________

____

Disadvantages

0 Online classes are bad because students can't ask teachers questions in person.

I think that they are not practical.

2 ____________

____

LESSON 4

문장의 확장 II

UNIT 1 주격 관계대명사
UNIT 2 목적격 관계대명사

model car	delicious	remember	sommelier
gym	hat	look for	barista
hamster	strawberry	respect	curator
fur	fruit	cartoon	support
hairdresser	joy	place	trust
remote control	pleasure	trail	lose
thief	doll	traditional	actor
run away	laptop	temple	leave
steal	receive	artwork	practice
baker	order	error	in front of

UNIT 1 주격 관계대명사

I am a nice person **who** prepares Christmas presents for friends.

★ 관계대명사가 이끄는 절은 앞에 나온 명사(선행사)를 수식하는 역할을 한다. 절 속에서 주어 역할을 하는 주격 관계대명사는 선행사가 사람일 때는 who, 사물이나 동물일 때는 which를 쓴다.

I have *a classmate* **who** enjoys making model cars.
The gym **which** is near my house is good.
Mike has *a hamster* **which** is very cute.

A

다음 두 문장을 who 또는 which로 연결하여 한 문장으로 쓰시오.

1 Taemin has some friends. They want to be singers.

2 Steve has a cat. It has black fur.

3 The man lives next door. He is a hairdresser.

4 Julie wants to buy the pants. They have big pockets.

5 Pass me the remote control. It is on the sofa.

6 The restaurant was good. It opened last Friday.

7 Ben is the boy. He won first prize.

8 I bought a monitor. It has a big screen.

9 The thief ran away. He stole money.

Tips for Writing

주격 관계대명사 뒤의 동사는 선행사에 수를 일치시킨다.

B 각 보기에서 알맞은 표현을 찾아 우리말에 맞게 영어로 쓰시오.

roses a fruit the girl a baker the boy a blog the student

basketball a blue hat a lot of pictures delicious cakes from Spain a lot of vitamin C sweet

1 Susie는 스페인 출신인 학생을 안다.

2 Eric은 많은 사진이 있는 블로그를 가지고 있다.

3 Marie는 맛있는 케이크를 만드는 제빵사이다.

4 내 남자친구는 나에게 달콤한 향기가 나는 장미들을 사주었다.

5 파란 모자를 쓰고 있는 소녀가 나의 가장 친한 친구이다.

6 딸기는 많은 비타민 C를 가지고 있는 과일이다.

7 Harry는 농구를 매우 잘하는 소년이다.

C 괄호 안의 표현을 활용하여 친구들이 만나고 싶어하는 유명인사에 대해 쓰시오.

0

(not have arms and legs / hope)

Jiyeon wants to meet the famous speaker Nick Vujicic.

He is the speaker who doesn't have arms and legs.

He is a man who gives people hope.

1

(write the *Harry Potter* series / joy)

Ron wants to meet the famous writer J. K. Rowling.

1)

2)

2

(donate money to poor people / pleasure)

Binna wants to meet the famous singer Kim Janghun.

1)

2)

UNIT 2 목적격 관계대명사

*I wear the big shoes **which** my father gave me.*

★ 관계대명사가 절 속에서 목적어 역할을 할 때 목적격 관계대명사를 쓰는데 선행사가 사람일 때는 whom, 사물이나 동물인 경우에는 which를 쓴다.

The girl **who(m)** Alex likes is my friend.
I know the boy **who(m)** Jessica is talking to.
This is the smartphone **which** I bought yesterday.
The doll store **which** I visited yesterday was very big.

Note
목적격 관계대명사 whom 대신 who를 쓰는 경우가 많다.

A

다음 두 문장을 whom 또는 which로 연결하여 한 문장으로 쓰시오.

1 My teacher liked the essay. Peter wrote it.

2 Jason Mraz is the singer. I wanted to see him.

3 This is the talk show. Kevin watches it on Fridays.

4 This is the boy. Jiyeon talked about him yesterday.

5 Potato pizza is the food. Sue likes it the most.

6 Tell me about the story. You heard it today.

7 The man was my math teacher. I saw him on the street.

8 The laptop doesn't work. My brother bought it last week.

9 The doctor was very kind to me. I saw her yesterday.

B 보기에서 알맞은 표현을 찾아 우리말에 맞게 영어로 쓰시오.

look for
bake
travel with
remember
order
cartoon show
respect
take

1 나는 내가 지난주에 주문했던 책들을 받지 못했다.

2 Emily는 그녀가 브라질에서 만났던 사람들을 기억한다.

3 Julie는 우리가 지난 토요일에 찍었던 사진들을 가지고 있다.

4 내가 함께 여행했던 사람들은 친절했다.

5 Sam이 구웠던 그 쿠키들은 정말로 맛있었다.

6 Ms. Song은 우리가 존경하는 선생님이시다.

7 이것이 Jenny가 찾고 있었던 열쇠이다.

8 The Simpsons는 내가 가장 좋아하는 만화이다.

C 괄호 안의 단어를 활용하여 여행지를 추천하는 문장을 쓰시오.

0 

(Jeju / a hiking trail)

The place which I recommend is Jeju.

Jeju has a hiking trail which many people visit.

1 

(Yongin / a traditional area)

1)

2)

2 

(Gyeongju / a temple)

1)

2)

WRAP UP

A

그림을 보고 각 보기의 표현을 활용하여 직업을 설명하는 문장을 쓰시오.

0  1  2  3 

take care of the artwork	find errors	make coffee

a museum	a coffee shop	new games

0 A sommelier is a person who provides wine service in a restaurant.

1 A barista ______________________.

2 A curator ______________________.

3 A game tester ______________________.

B

주어진 표현을 활용하여 친구들이 가장 좋아하는 운동과 팀에 대해 쓰시오.

0
- David
- baseball
- the New York Yankees

Baseball is the sport which David likes the most.

The team which he supports is the New York Yankees.

1
- Alice
- soccer
- Manchester United

1) ______________________

2) ______________________

2
- Harry
- basketball
- the LA Lakers

1) ______________________

2) ______________________

C 다음 우리말에 맞게 영어로 쓰시오.

1

Jake는 그를 도와줄 수 있는 누군가를 찾고 있다. (look for, someone)

2

이것이 나의 엄마가 가지길 원하시는 그 가방이다.

3

Jim은 내가 믿을 수 있는 친구이다. (trust)

4

나는 나의 아빠가 나에게 주신 그 시계를 잃어버렸다.

5

선글라스를 쓰고 있는 그 남자는 유명한 배우이다. (sunglasses)

6

서울로 가는 기차는 두 시에 떠난다.

7

내가 오늘 아침에 잃어버렸던 지갑은 파란색이었다.

D 다음 우리말에 맞게 영어로 쓰시오.

1

1) 나는 올랜도에서 살고 있는 나의 삼촌을 방문했다. He took me to the Disneyland. I rode a lot of exciting rides there. 2) 나는 내가 좋아하는 디즈니 캐릭터들을 보았다. I was very happy.

1) ______ (Orlando)

2) ______ (Disney characters)

2

We are the school band, Cross. 1) 우리는 노래를 매우 잘하는 소녀를 찾고 있습니다. If you are interested, 2) Student Union 건물에 있는 우리의 연습실을 방문해주세요.

1) ______

2) ______ (practice room)

E 주어진 정보를 바탕으로 맛집을 소개하는 글을 쓰시오.

1

Place – Café On
Location – next to the movie theater
Menu – fruit juice **Taste** – very fresh

I recommend Café On which 1) ________________ . (location)

They sell fruit juice 2) ________________ . (taste)

2

Place – Dragon
Location – in front of the NE school
Menu – *tteokbokki* **Taste** – very spicy

1) ________________

2) ________________

F 다음 그림을 보고, 괄호 안의 단어를 활용하여 공원에 있는 등장인물들의 행동을 묘사한 문장을 쓰시오.

There are some people at the park.

0 Look at the dog which is playing with a little boy . (play)

1 There is a little boy ________________ . (kick)

2 A girl is talking to a boy ________________ . (wear)

3 A woman is sitting next to a man ________________ . (listen)

SECTION 2

GRAMMAR FOR WRITING

LESSON 5

시제

UNIT 1 미래시제
UNIT 2 현재완료

report	practice	ballet	art
on time	since	vacation	painting
memorize	several	prepare	then
sale	series	heavily	history
department store	kangaroo	late	university
soon	glasses	keep in touch	keyboard
online class	win	move	electric
climb	prize	remember	bathe
save	contest	forever	camel
plan	competition	again	race

UNIT 1 미래시제

I am **going to go** to the jungle for this holiday.
I **will make** many animal friends there.

1 '~일 것이다'라는 의미로 미래의 일을 예측할 때 〈will + 동사원형〉 또는 〈be going to + 동사원형〉을 쓴다.
It **will snow** on Christmas Day. It **is going to snow** on Christmas Day.

2 '~하겠다'라는 의미로 주어의 의지를 표현할 때 〈will + 동사원형〉을 쓴다.
I **will finish** this report tonight. I **will help** you carry these boxes.

3 '~할 예정이다'라는 의미로 이미 결정된 계획을 표현할 때 〈be going to + 동사원형〉을 쓴다.
We **are going to go** skiing this weekend.
He **is going to take** a swimming class this summer.

A 괄호 안의 표현을 활용하여 문장을 다음과 같이 고쳐 쓰시오.

0 Brian plays basketball. (be going to, this Sunday)
Brian is going to play basketball this Sunday.

1 The weather is fine. (will, this weekend)

2 Joe visits his uncle. (be going to, tomorrow)

3 I lend you my laptop. (will)

4 We arrive on time. (be going to)

5 I memorize fifty English words every day. (will)

6 The singer has a concert. (be going to, next month)

7 There is a big sale at the department store. (will, soon)

Tips for Writing
조동사 뒤의 동사에는 -(e)s를 붙이지 않는다.

B

그림을 보고 각 보기에서 알맞은 표현을 찾아 이번 주말 계획에 대한 문장을 쓰시오.

0 

1 

2 

3 

take	climb	learn

Mt. Dobong	jazz dance	an online class

0 Taehwan *is going to go camping this weekend*.

1 Anne ______________________.

2 Brian ______________________.

3 Bobae ______________________.

C

주어진 표현을 활용하여 나의 계획에 대해 쓰시오.

0
- take an English test
- next week
- study English hard

I am going to take an English test next week.

I will study English hard for it.

1
- buy a jacket
- next month
- save money

1) ______________________

2) ______________________

2
- take a trip to Egypt
- this summer
- make a plan

1) ______________________

2) ______________________

3
- have a dance audition
- next week
- practice hard

1) ______________________

2) ______________________

UNIT 2 현재완료

We **have walked** for days.
But don't worry. I **have been** to Hula-Hula-Town before.
We will be there soon.

★ 과거의 일이 현재와 관련 있을 때 〈have + v-ed〉 형태의 현재완료를 쓴다. 주로 '~한 적이 있다'라는 의미로 현재까지의 경험, 또는 '(지금까지 계속) ~해 왔다'라는 의미로 과거에서 현재까지 계속되는 일을 나타낼 때 쓴다.

I **have eaten** Vietnamese food before.
Kate **has** never **been** to New York.
I **have lived** in Seoul for ten years.
Joe **has had** a cat since he was young.

Note
현재완료와 함께 잘 쓰이는 표현
1 경험: before(전에), once(한 번), twice(두 번), three times(세 번), never(한 번도 ~않다)
2 계속: for(~동안), since(~이래로)

A 괄호 안의 표현을 활용하여 문장을 다음과 같이 고쳐 쓰시오.

0 My uncle lives in Beijing. (since 2005)
My uncle has lived in Beijing since 2005.

1 I never eat pizza at this restaurant. (before)

2 Linda likes to sing. (since she was young)

3 Inho sleeps. (for ten hours)

4 We play this game. (once)

5 Julia and Soobin are friends. (for three years)

6 Kelly goes to Minji's house. (several times)

7 Jinsu learns Judo. (for six months)

B 보기에서 알맞은 단어를 찾아 우리말에 맞게 영어로 쓰시오.

sick
kangaroos
Chinese
Jejudo
the *Twilight* series
golf
glasses

1 나는 트와일라잇 시리즈를 두 번 읽은 적이 있다.

2 June은 어제부터 아프다.

3 나는 호주에서 캥거루들을 본 적이 있다.

4 Sophie는 그녀가 8살 때부터 안경을 썼다.

5 Maria는 골프를 쳐본 적이 없다.

6 Tony는 2년 동안 중국어를 공부해 왔다.

7 나는 제주도에 세 번 가 본 적이 있다.

C 괄호 안의 표현을 활용하여 상을 받은 친구를 소개하는 문장을 쓰시오.

0 

(study Korean, five years / Korean speech contest, once)

Amy has studied Korean for five years.

She has won a prize at the Korean speech contest once.

1 

(swim, two years / swimming competition, twice)

1) Amanda ______.

2) ______

2 

(do ballet, seven years / ballet contest, three times)

1) David ______.

2) ______

WRAP UP

A 괄호 안의 표현을 활용하여 방학 계획에 대한 질문에 알맞은 대답을 쓰시오.

1 What is your plan for this vacation? (take a trip to Italy)

I am going ______________________.

2 Is this your first trip to Italy? (never, be)

Yes, it is. I ______________________.

3 When are you going to leave? (on July 15th)

____

4 How long have you prepared for the trip? (a month)

____

5 Where are you going to go in Italy? (the Colosseum in Rome)

____

B 그림을 보고 괄호 안의 표현을 활용하여 친구들의 능력에 대한 문장을 쓰시오.

0 

1 

2 

3 

0 Sally can play chess.

She has played chess many times. (play, many times)

1 Jongmin cannot play the flute.

______________________ (never, learn to play)

2 Suyoung can speak Chinese.

______________________ (study, she was nine)

3 Max can do taekwondo.

______________________ (learn, seven years)

C 다음 우리말에 맞게 영어로 쓰시오.

1

나는 올해 12권의 책을 읽을 것이다.

2

이번 주말에 비가 심하게 내릴 것이다. (heavily)

3

Jessica는 그 영화를 열 번 본 적이 있다.

4

나는 이 휴대전화를 3년 동안 사용해 왔다.

5

우리는 30분 늦게 도착할 것이다. (thirty minutes late)

6

나는 다음 달에 권투수업을 받을 예정이다. (boxing lessons)

7

나의 가족은 한 번 디즈니랜드에 가본 적이 있다. (Disneyland)

D 다음 우리말에 맞게 영어로 쓰시오.

1

Dear Hyejin,
1) 나는 이번 주말에 이사 할 예정이야. I am sad but 2) 나는 너를 영원히 기억할 거야. Let's keep in touch. I hope to see you again.

1) ______________________ (move)

2) ______________________ (forever)

2

1) 나는 파리에 두 번 가본 적이 있다. I went to some art galleries there, and I saw many paintings. 2) 나는 그때 이후로 미술을 좋아해 왔다. I want to study art history in university.

1) ______________________

2) ______________________ (then)

E

주어진 정보를 바탕으로 밴드 멤버를 소개하는 글을 쓰시오.

0 

Jake *Our Keyboardist!*

(piano, seven years / keyboard, 2012)

He has played the piano for seven years.
He has played the keyboard in our band since 2012.

1 

John *Our Drummer!*

(drums, three years / drums, 2011)

1) ______________________

2) ______________________

2 

Emily *Our Guitarist!*

(guitar, five years / electric guitar, 2010)

1) ______________________

2) ______________________

F

자신의 해외 여행 경험 중 가장 기억에 남는 것에 대해 다음 내용을 포함하여 쓰시오.

- the place which you went to
- the activity which you did

0 I have been to India. (India)

I have bathed in the Ganges. (in the Ganges)

1 1) ______________________ (Qatar)

2) ______________________ (a camel race)

2 1) ______________________ (Switzerland)

2) ______________________ (an open cable car)

LESSON 6

수동태

UNIT 1 수동태의 기본 형태
UNIT 2 by 이외의 전치사를 사용하는 수동태

hold	fortress	beauty	repair
police officer	theater	dangerous	dust
release	ghost	pajama	cultural
company	satisfy	cotton	icon
recommend	fill	lambskin	tourist
mirror	piggy bank	leather	pack
designer	indeed	direct	including
purse	interest	novel	parade
locate	result	compose	amazing
tomb	surprise	piece	chest

UNIT 1 수동태의 기본 형태

I won't **be caught** by you.

★ '~가 …당하다[받다]'라는 의미로 주어가 행위의 영향을 받는 대상임을 표현할 때 〈be동사 + v-ed〉 형태의 수동태를 쓴다. 행위자를 나타낼 때에는 보통 〈by + 행위자〉를 쓴다.

Pororo **is loved** by many children.
The first Olympics **were held** in Athens.
The restaurant **will be closed** next Monday.

Note

1 행위자가 막연한 일반인 또는 분명하지 않거나 중요하지 않을 때 〈by + 행위자〉는 보통 생략한다.

2 미래의 수동태는 〈will be + v-ed〉이고, 과거의 수동태는 〈be동사의 과거형 + v-ed〉로 쓴다.

A

문장을 다음과 같이 고쳐 쓰시오.

0 Many people visit Tina's blog.
Tina's blog is visited by many people.

1 The police officer caught the thief.

2 They will release the new movie next Friday.

3 Many people all over the world drink Coca-Cola.

4 A Korean company made this 3D TV.

5 I will cook dinner on Parents' Day.

6 Many people read the *Harry Potter* series.

7 Peter took these pictures of babies.

8 My friends recommended this restaurant.

B 각 보기에서 알맞은 표현을 찾아 우리말에 맞게 영어로 쓰시오

one's purse the mirror these cookies many children a famous designer many fans the package smartphones

design use love break read steal bake deliver

1 그 가수는 많은 팬들에게 사랑받는다.

2 이 쿠키들은 Jessica에 의해 구워졌다.

3 그 거울은 어제 Jason에 의해 깨졌다.

4 스마트폰은 많은 사람들에 의해 사용된다.

5 이 드레스는 유명한 디자이너에 의해 디자인되었다.

6 그 소포는 곧 배달될 것이다.

7 내 지갑은 어제 지하철에서 도난당했다.

8 이 책은 많은 어린이들에게 읽힌다.

C 주어진 정보를 활용하여 세계의 신비로운 건축물에 대해 쓰시오.

0
- the Pyramids, Egypt
- 2550 B.C.
- a tomb for the king

The Pyramids are located in Egypt.
They were built in 2550 B.C.
They were used as a tomb for the king.

1
- the Great Wall, China
- the 7th century B.C.
- a fortress

1)
2)
3)

2
- the Colosseum, Italy
- 80 A.D.
- a theater

1)
2)
3)

UNIT 2 by 이외의 전치사를 사용하는 수동태

I am interested in baking cookies for my friends.

1 수동태 문장에서 행위자는 보통 by를 써서 나타내지만, 다른 전치사를 쓰기도 한다.

The road **was covered with** leaves.

Chocolate **is made from** cacao.

2 '~라고들 말한다'라는 의미로 people say that ~의 수동태인 ⟨it is said that ~⟩을 쓴다.

It is said that a ghost lives in this house.

It is said that the food in this restaurant is good.

Note

be interested in: ~에 흥미가 있다
be covered with: ~로 덮여있다
be made of[from]: ~로 만들어지다
be filled with: ~로 가득 채워지다
be concerned with: ~에 관계가 있다
be satisfied with: ~에 만족하다
be surprised at: ~에 놀라다

A 문장을 다음과 같이 고쳐 쓰시오.

0 My answer satisfied my English teacher.

My English teacher was satisfied with my answer.

1 A brown carpet covers the floor.

2 People say that the movie is boring.

3 Coins fill this red piggy bank.

4 People say that a friend in need is a friend indeed.

5 Figure skating interests my sister.

6 The result of the game surprised people.

7 People say that the story is true.

B 보기에서 알맞은 표현을 찾아 우리말에 맞게 영어로 쓰시오.

playing golf
onions and carrots
the beauty of Bali
the Olympic games
one's service
rich
dangerous
strawberries

1 그 케이크는 딸기들로 덮여 있었다.

2 모든 뉴스가 올림픽 경기들과 관련이 있다.

3 나의 엄마는 그들의 서비스에 만족해하셨다.

4 Mr. Johnson이 매우 부자라고들 말한다.

5 Jane은 발리의 아름다움에 놀랐다.

6 그 산은 위험하다고들 말한다.

7 나의 아빠는 골프 치는 것에 관심이 있으시다.

8 이 수프는 양파와 당근으로 만들어졌다.

C 주어진 표현을 활용하여 제품을 설명하는 문장을 쓰시오.

0 
- pajamas
- cotton
- good for our skin

These pajamas are made of cotton.

It is said that cotton is good for our skin.

1 
- coat
- goose down
- keep us warm

1)

2)

2 
- shoes
- lambskin
- softer than leather

1)

2)

WRAP UP

A

주어진 정보를 활용하여 여러 가지 작품에 대해 쓰시오.

0 movie: *Transformers*
director: Michael Bay
Transformers was directed by Michael Bay.

1 novel: *Twilight*
writer: Stephenie Meyer
....

2 picture: The *Mona Lisa*
painter: Leonardo da Vinci
....

3 composition: *Wedding March*
composer: Richard Wagner
....

4 piece: *The Thinker*
maker: Auguste Rodin
....

B

그림을 보고 괄호 안의 단어를 활용하여 신발가게에서 일어난 일에 대해 쓰시오.

0 

1 

2 

3 

Bora went to a shoe store downtown.

0 *The shoe store was filled with people.* (fill)

1 .... (interest)

2 She saw the tag. It says that .... (make)

3 The price was $1,000. .... (surprise)

C 다음 우리말에 맞게 영어로 쓰시오.

1

우리 교실은 매일 청소된다.

2

그 놀이공원은 많은 사람들로 가득 찼다. (amusement park)

3

그 컴퓨터는 나의 형에 의해 고쳐졌다. (repair)

4

그 책들은 먼지로 덮여 있었다. (dust)

5

이 돈은 아픈 사람들을 위해 쓰여질 것이다.

6

인도의 왕이 그의 아내를 위해 타지마할을 지었다고들 말한다. (Taj Mahal)

7

Ron은 그 시험 결과에 만족했다. (test result)

D 다음 우리말에 맞게 영어로 쓰시오.

1

The Eiffel Tower is a cultural icon in Paris. 1) 그 탑은 1889년에 지어졌다. 2) 그것은 Gustave Eiffel에 의해 디자인되었다. It is the tallest tower in Paris now. It is visited by many tourists every year.

1) ______

2) ______

2

1) 나의 아빠와 나는 산을 오르는 데 흥미가 있다. We are going to climb Mt. Jili this weekend. 2) 현재 지리산은 눈으로 덮여있다고 한다. So we should pack many things including snow chains.

1) ______

2) ______

E 주어진 정보를 바탕으로 세계 축제에 관한 글을 쓰시오.

1

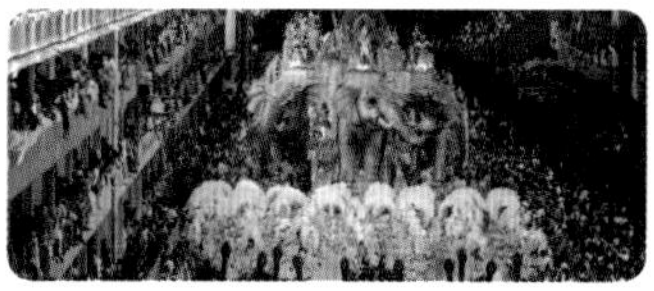

· The Rio Samba Carnival, Brazil
· Started: about 290 years ago
· Things to see: the samba parade, fun

1) The Rio Samba Carnival __________________ in Brazil. (hold)

2) It __________________________________. (start)

3) It __________________ the samba parade is fun. (say)

2

· Oktoberfest, Germany
· Started: about 200 years ago
· Things to see: the many kinds of beer, amazing

1) __________________________________

2) __________________________________

3) __________________________________

F 다음 그림을 보고 괄호 안의 단어를 활용하여 세진이의 방을 묘사한 문장을 쓰시오.

This is Sejin's room.

1 The desk __________________________________. (cover)

2 The box under the desk __________________________. (fill)

3 The chest under the picture ________________________. (make)

LESSON 7

조동사

UNIT 1 요청을 나타내는 could, would
UNIT 2 의무를 나타내는 must, have to

favor	right	dormitory	bright
pass	brush	lock	outside
air conditioner	tooth	check out	sunscreen
turn on	apologize	fold	rice
turn off	promise	turn down	follow
take a break	dentist	volume	wrap up
order	careful	allergic	potluck party
airport	motorcycle	peanut	costume
hang	slippery	due	rehearse
fasten	within	traffic light	exhibition

UNIT 1 요청을 나타내는 could, would

★ '~해주시겠어요?'라는 의미로 정중하게 요청할 때 could나 would를 쓴다. could는 권유를 나타낼 때에도 쓸 수 있다.

Could you do me a favor?
Could you tell me the time?
Would you lend me your English textbook?
If you are hungry, you **could** have some sandwiches.

Note
could는 can보다, would는 will보다 더 정중하고 공손한 요청을 나타낸다.

A 괄호 안의 단어를 배열하여 올바른 문장으로 다시 쓰시오.

1 제게 그 책을 건네주시겠어요? (book, the, pass, you, would, me)

2 조용히 해주시겠어요? (you, be, could, quiet)

3 여기에 서명해주시겠어요? (would, here, sign, you)

4 제 숙제를 도와주시겠어요? (help, my, with, homework, you, could, me)

5 제게 당신의 성함을 말씀해주시겠어요? (me, you, would, your, tell, name)

6 제게 당신의 신분증을 보여주시겠어요? (your, could, ID, me, you, show)

7 제게 물을 좀 주시겠어요? (give, you, would, water, some, me)

8 당신의 카메라를 가져와 주시겠어요? (your, bring, could, camera, you)

9 너무 더우시면 에어컨을 켜세요. (air conditioner, could, turn, you, the, on)
If it is too hot, ____________________

Tips for Writing
요청을 나타내는 could나 would로 시작하는 문장의 끝에는 물음표(?)를 쓴다.

B 보기에서 알맞은 표현을 찾아 우리말에 맞게 영어로 쓰시오.

recommend
take a break
fix
speak
lend
turn off
close

1 당신의 펜을 저에게 빌려주시겠어요?

2 그 문을 닫아주시겠어요?

3 당신의 휴대전화를 꺼주시겠어요?

4 책 한 권을 추천해주시겠어요?

5 제 자전거를 고쳐주시겠어요?

6 천천히 말씀해주시겠어요?

7 당신이 피곤하면 쉬세요.

C 그림을 보고 각 보기에서 알맞은 표현을 찾아 상황에 적절한 문장을 쓰시오.

drive	hang	fasten	hold

one's seat belt	this picture	to the airport	this chair

0

Customer: *Could you take my order?*

Clerk: *Sure, would you tell me your address?*

1

Woman: 1) ______ on the wall?

Man: 2) Sure, ______?

2

Customer: 1) ______

Taxi driver: 2) ______

UNIT 2 의무를 나타내는 must, have to

*When we receive a gift, we **must open** it right away.*

★ '~해야 한다'라는 의미로 의무를 표현할 때 ⟨must + 동사원형⟩ 또는 ⟨have to + 동사원형⟩을 쓴다.

We **must save** energy.

Dan **has to clean** the classroom this afternoon.

Julie **had to study** last night.

Note

must의 과거형은 had to이다.

A 문장을 다음과 같이 고쳐 쓰시오.

0 You brush your teeth after a meal.

You have to brush your teeth after a meal.

1 I finish my report.

2 Tom apologizes to me first.

3 My father worked late last night.

4 We keep our promises.

5 Soobin goes to the dentist.

6 Henry got up early this morning.

7 You are careful with the knife.

8 Laura helps her grandmother this weekend.

9 Yuna changed trains at City Hall station.

B 표지판을 보고 각 보기에서 알맞은 표현을 찾아 상황에 맞게 안내문을 쓰시오.

0 

1 

2 

3 

turn off	walk	wear

one's cell phone	a helmet	carefully

0 Because this is a school zone, you must drive slowly .

1 When you ride a motorcycle, ____________ .

2 While the movie is playing, ____________ .

3 Because the floor is slippery, ____________ .

C 주어진 표현과 보기의 단어를 활용하여 각 장소에 알맞은 규칙을 쓰시오.

return	lock	come back	check out

0
- within two weeks
- one's library card

Library Rules

You must return books within two weeks.

You must show your library card when you borrow a book.

1
- by 10:00 p.m.
- one's door

Dormitory Rules

1) ____________

2) ____________ when you leave.

2
- by 11:00 a.m.
- one's hotel key

Hotel Rules

1) ____________

2) ____________ before you leave.

WRAP UP

A 다음은 지하철 안의 모습이다. 괄호 안의 단어를 이용하여 그림 속 인물에게 적절한 부탁을 쓰시오.

0 Could you give your seat to the old lady? (give)

1 .... (speak)

2 .... (fold)

3 .... (turn down)

B 각 보기에서 알맞은 표현을 찾아 주어진 상황에서 해야 할 일에 대한 문장을 쓰시오.

wear	take	return	cross

the street	these books	pictures	sunscreen

0 You are allergic to peanuts. You must not eat peanuts.

1 These books are due today. ....

2 The traffic light is red. ....

3 The sun is too bright outside. ....

4 Look at the "No photos" sign. ....

C 다음 우리말에 맞게 영어로 쓰시오.

1

저에게 밥을 더 주시겠어요? (rice)

2

우리는 그 학교 규칙들을 따라야 한다. (follow)

3

제 가방을 봐 주시겠어요? (watch)

4

나는 어제 Katie에게 이메일 한 통을 보내야 했다.

5

저에게 메뉴판을 가져다 주시겠어요? (menu)

6

John은 이번 토요일에 학교에 가야 한다.

7

제 우산을 빌려 가세요. (borrow)

D 다음 우리말에 맞게 영어로 쓰시오.

1

Jinho: 1) 저희 엄마를 위한 선물을 추천해주시겠어요?
Clerk: How about this lipstick? It is very popular.
Jinho: Oh, that is good. 2) 그 선물을 포장해 주시겠어요?

1) .... (recommend)

2) .... (wrap up)

2

My English teacher gave me homework yesterday. 1) 나는 어젯밤에 내 숙제를 해야 했다. But I didn't do it. So 2) 나는 오늘 오후에 교실을 청소해야 한다. That is our class rule.

1) ....

2) ....

E 다음은 파티의 초대장이다. 주어진 정보를 바탕으로 초대장을 쓰시오.

0	- housewarming party - bring food / potluck party	Date: July 10th, 6:00 p.m. Place: At Minjun's house Could you come to the housewarming party? You must bring food because it is a potluck party.
1	- birthday party - keep it secret / surprise party	Date: March 15th, 1:00 p.m. Place: At the Family Restaurant 1) ____________ 2) ____________
2	- Halloween party - wear interesting clothes / costume party	Date: October 30th, 7:00 p.m. Place: At the Steve's house 1) ____________ 2) ____________

F 친구가 방과 후에 쇼핑을 가자고 하는데 이를 거절해야 하는 상황이다. 다음에 제시된 그림을 보고, 주어진 어구를 활용하여 거절하는 메시지를 쓰시오.

0

- the drama club meeting
- rehearse for the play

1

- home
- go to one's piano lesson

2

- the science exhibition
- do science homework

0 I am sorry, but I must go to the drama club meeting.

I have to rehearse for the play.

1 1) ____________

2) ____________

2 1) ____________

2) ____________

LESSON 8

to부정사와 동명사

UNIT 1 형용사적 용법의 to부정사
UNIT 2 부사적 용법의 to부정사
UNIT 3 to부정사 vs. 동명사

hide	rude	package	oversleep
kid	bottle	fence	go off
toy	habit	get into	set
solve	password	through	alarm clock
look for	go out	convenience	get to
disappoint	heat up	audition	view
raise	light	do one's best	circus
pleased	notebook	ring	artwork
receive	stationery	doorbell	pot
living room	account	worried	lantern

UNIT 1 형용사적 용법의 to부정사

We have our secret place **to hide** in.

★ '~하는'이라는 의미로 to부정사가 형용사처럼 명사를 수식할 수 있다. 이 때 to부정사는 수식하는 명사 뒤에 쓴다.

I have *some pictures* **to show** you.

Sean bought *something* **to drink**.

The kid has *many toys* **to play** with.

Note

〈동사 + 전치사〉의 동사구를 to부정사로 쓸 때 전치사를 빠뜨리지 않도록 주의한다.

A **괄호 안의 단어를 배열하여 올바른 문장으로 다시 쓰시오.**

1 우리는 먹을 것을 주문했다. (eat, something, to, ordered, we)

2 나의 가족은 앉을 큰 소파가 필요하다.
(to, family, needs, big, on, sofa, sit, a, my)

3 이것은 풀기 쉬운 문제이다. (easy, to, this, an, question, is, solve)

4 그들은 살 집을 가지고 있지 않다. (a, they, live, have, to, in, house, don't)

5 나는 네게 말할 것이 있다. (something, have, tell, I, to, you)

6 그녀는 그 파티에서 입을 드레스를 샀다.
(dress, at, party, bought, the, wear, she, to, a)

7 John은 함께 이야기할 누군가가 없다. (anyone, John, talk, have, doesn't, to, with)

8 Mike는 장난감을 넣을 상자가 필요하다. (a, toys, Mike, box, put, needs, in, to)

B 보기에서 알맞은 표현을 찾아 우리말에 맞게 영어로 쓰시오.

exercise play with write with look for a comic book

1 Brian은 기차에서 읽을 만화책을 한 권 샀다.

2 Ruby는 나에게 쓸 펜을 빌려주었다.

3 나는 내 여자친구에게 줄 선물을 찾고 있다.

4 Max는 운동할 충분한 시간이 필요하다.

5 그 소년들은 가지고 놀 공을 원했다.

UNIT 2 부사적 용법의 to부정사

The policeman climbed ladders ***to catch*** *Pippi.*

★ '~하기 위해'라는 의미로 어떤 행동의 이유나 목적을 표현하고자 할 때, 또는 '~해서'라는 의미로 감정의 원인을 표현할 때 to부정사를 쓸 수 있다.

Ron saved some money **to buy** a tablet PC.
I watch American dramas **to learn** English.
I am so glad **to see** you again.
Harry was disappointed **to lose** the soccer game.

A 괄호 안의 단어를 배열하여 올바른 문장으로 다시 쓰시오.

1 나는 제시간에 도착하기 위해 택시를 탔다. (taxi, a, I, arrive, on time, took, to)

2 John은 Tom을 만나서 놀랐다. (surprised, John, meet, to, Tom, was)

3 나는 질문을 하기 위해 손을 들었다. (a, ask, hand, my, raised, I, to, question)

4 Max는 우유를 사기 위해 가게로 갔다. (Max, to, went, the, milk, buy, to, store)

5 그녀는 그 선물을 받아서 기뻤다. (pleased, she, receive, the, was, to, present)

B **보기에서 알맞은 표현을 찾아 우리말에 맞게 영어로 쓰시오.**

the rude people
secret
the living room
pass
some bread
a gold medal

1 Mary는 그녀의 엄마를 돕기 위해 거실을 청소했다.

2 Usain은 금메달을 따서 행복했다.

3 Jerry는 샌드위치를 만들기 위해 빵을 좀 샀다.

4 내 여동생은 그 시험에 합격하기 위해 열심히 공부했다.

5 나는 그 무례한 사람들을 봐서 화났다.

6 우리는 그를 놀라게 하기 위해 파티를 비밀로 유지했다.

UNIT 3 to부정사 vs. 동명사

I **try to be** happy at school because vacation will start soon.

★ to부정사와 동명사 모두를 목적어로 취하지만 각각의 의미가 다른 동사가 있다.

1 ⟨remember v-ing⟩ ~한 것을 기억하다
Ash **remembers locking** the door.
⟨remember to-v⟩ ~할 것을 기억하다
I **remembered to do** homework.

2 ⟨forget v-ing⟩ ~한 것을 잊다
I **forgot lending** Amy the money.
⟨forget to-v⟩ ~할 것을 잊다
He **forgot to bring** his wallet.

3 ⟨try v-ing⟩ (시험 삼아) ~해보다
I **tried calling** Dan.
⟨try to-v⟩ ~하려고 노력하다
Jason **tried to open** the bottle.

A 보기에서 알맞은 표현을 찾아 우리말에 맞게 영어로 쓰시오.

meet
memorize
put
one's bad habits
return
the dentist
see
password

1 나는 뉴욕에서 Ben을 본 것을 기억한다.

....

2 그는 그의 나쁜 습관들을 바꾸려고 노력했다.

....

3 Lisa는 테이블 위에 그 열쇠를 둔 것을 잊어버렸다.

....

4 Kelly는 Eva를 만날 것을 기억했다.

....

5 나는 그 문을 열기 위해 다른 비밀번호를 사용해봤다.

....

6 Emily는 치과에 갈 것을 기억했다.

....

7 그녀는 그 책들을 오늘 반납할 것을 잊어버렸다.

....

8 Andy는 그들의 이름들을 외우려고 노력했다.

....

B 엄마가 남긴 메모이다. 주어진 표현을 활용하여 해야 할 일에 대한 문장을 쓰시오.

0
- do one's homework
- come home

Remember to do your homework before you go out.

Don't forget to come home before nine o'clock.

1
- heat up the pizza
- do the dishes

1) .... before you eat it.

2) .... after you eat.

2
- turn off the light
- lock the door

1) .... before you go out.

2) .... when you go out.

WRAP UP

A

그림을 보고 괄호 안의 표현을 활용하여 현지가 오늘 할 일에 대한 문장을 쓰시오.

0 
1 
2 
3 

0 (a notebook, write in / stationery store, buy one)

Hyunji needs a notebook to write in. She will go to the stationery store to buy one.

1 (a savings account, put money in / bank, open one)

....

2 (a package, send / post office, send it)

....

3 (some milk, drink / supermarket, buy some)

....

B

그림을 보고 괄호 안의 단어를 활용하여 질문에 알맞은 대답을 쓰시오.

0 Did the thief climb over the fence?

No, he didn't. He tried to climb over the fence. But he couldn't. (try)

1 Did the thief get into the house through the window?

Yes, he did. .... (try)

2 Did you lock the door when you left?

Yes, I did. .... (remember)

3 Did you close the window?

No, I didn't. .... (forget)

C 다음 우리말에 맞게 영어로 쓰시오.

1

나는 편의점에서 먹을 것을 샀다. (convenience store)

2

Susie는 그녀의 가방에 그녀의 휴대전화를 둔 것을 잊어버렸다.

3

Jack은 그의 수학 교과서를 가지고 오는 것을 잊어버렸다. (math textbook)

4

Ron은 그 오디션에 합격해서 행복했다. (pass)

5

공항에서 나에게 전화할 것을 기억해라.

6

그들은 그 경기를 이기기 위해 최선을 다했다. (do one's best)

7

Paul은 그 병을 열어 보려고 시도했다.

D 다음 우리말에 맞게 영어로 쓰시오.

1

Soyoung felt sick this morning, so 1) 그녀는 조금 쉬기 위해 학교에 가지 않았다. While she was sleeping, someone rang the doorbell. It was her friend, Tim. 2) 그녀는 그를 보고 놀랐다. He came to see her because he was worried.

1) .... (get some rest)

2) ....

2

This morning, I overslept. The alarm clock didn't go off because 1) 나는 알람을 맞추는 것을 잊어버렸다. 2) 나는 학교에 제시간에 도착하려고 노력했다, but I was late. My teacher was angry.

1) .... (set the alarm)

2) .... (get to)

E 주어진 정보를 바탕으로 여행지 추천에 관한 글을 쓰시오.

0

- Thailand
- enjoy the beautiful beaches
- delicious food, eat
- ride an elephant

You should go to Thailand to enjoy the beautiful beaches.
There is a lot of delicious food to eat.
Tip: Remember to ride an elephant!

1

- China
- see the Great Wall
- great views, enjoy
- watch the amazing circus

1) ______________________

2) ______________________

3) Tip: ______________________

2

- France
- visit the art museums
- great artwork, see
- take a boat ride on the River Seine

1) ______________________

2) ______________________

3) Tip: ______________________

F 캠핑을 가려는 친구에게 꼭 챙겨야 할 것에 대해 조언하려고 한다. 다음 제시된 그림을 보고, 주어진 어구를 활용하여 조언하는 메시지를 쓰시오.

0

- a tent
- sleep in

1

- a pot
- cook in

2

- a lantern
- go out at night

0 Remember to bring a tent.

You will need a tent to sleep in.

1 1) ______________________

2) ______________________

2 1) ______________________

2) ______________________

LESSON 9

수식어

UNIT 1 현재분사 vs. 과거분사
UNIT 2 빈도부사

shocking	frighten	text message	film
be afraid of	scream	costume	prepare
fortunately	catch a cold	vampire	touched
fall	advice	pumpkin	try
angel	make a decision	princess	detective
hike	typhoon	at all	thrill
boil	clerk	almost	scary
grade	customer	burn	space
during	give up on	make a mistake	sci-fi
cheer for	dessert	from now on	simple

UNIT 1 현재분사 vs. 과거분사

A lot of **exciting** things happen to me every day.

★ 분사는 동사원형에 -ing(현재분사)나 -ed(과거분사)를 붙인 것으로, 형용사처럼 명사를 수식하거나 보어로 쓰이기도 한다.

1 '~하는, ~하고 있는'이라는 능동이나 진행의 의미를 표현할 때 현재분사를 쓴다.
Julie heard **shocking** news.
Sujin is afraid of the **barking** dog.
Traveling is **exciting** but **tiring**.

2 '~한, ~된'이라는 수동이나 완료의 의미를 표현할 때 과거분사를 쓴다.
Fortunately, I found my **stolen** bike.
There were a lot of **fallen** leaves on the street.
Jay was **bored** with the movie.

Note
감정을 나타내는 분사
현재분사는 '~한 감정을 느끼게 하는'의 의미로 보통 사물이 주어로 온다. 과거분사는 '~한 감정을 느끼는'의 의미로 보통 사람이 주어로 온다.

A 문장을 다음과 같이 고쳐 쓰시오.

0 The (surprise) child started crying.
The surprised child started crying.

1 The (sleep) baby looks like an angel.

2 Sumi was (tire) from a long hike.

3 We listened to the sound of the (fall) rain.

4 My team was (satisfy) with the result of the game.

5 Don't touch the (break) glass.

6 It is (excite) to make new friends.

B 각 보기에서 알맞은 표현을 찾아 우리말에 맞게 영어로 쓰시오.

interest break boil disappoint lose satisfy surprise

on the train fix at the news during class one's test grade at this restaurant watch

1 우리는 기차에서 삶은 계란들을 먹었다.

....

2 John의 시험 점수는 실망스러웠다.

....

3 나의 아빠가 부서진 의자를 고치셨다.

....

4 이 식당에 음식은 만족스럽다.

....

5 나는 침대 밑에서 내 잃어버린 시계를 찾았다.

....

6 사람들은 그 소식에 놀랐다.

....

7 우리 선생님께서 수업 중에 우리에게 재미있는 이야기를 말씀해주셨다.

....

C 그림을 보고 보기의 단어와 괄호 안의 표현을 활용하여 상황을 묘사하는 문장을 쓰시오.

frighten excite

0 

(concert / audience, leave the concert hall)

The concert was disappointing.

The disappointed audience left the concert hall.

1 

(baseball game / fans, cheer for the team)

1) ....

2) ....

2 

(horror movie / people, scream)

1) ....

2) ....

UNIT 2 빈도부사

I **often** go up on the roof to see the sunrise.
But my friends are **always** afraid of going up there.

★ 어떤 일이 얼마나 자주 일어나는지를 표현하는 빈도부사는 보통 일반동사 앞 또는 be동사나 조동사 뒤에 쓴다.

My mother **usually** *drinks* coffee in the morning.
Harry *is* **often** late for school.
I *will* **never** tell anyone your secret.

Note
빈도부사
always: 항상
usually: 대개, 보통
often: 종종, 자주
sometimes: 가끔, 때때로
never: 결코 ~ 않다

A 괄호 안의 단어를 배열하여 올바른 문장으로 다시 쓰시오.

1 James는 겨울에 자주 감기에 걸린다. (often, catches, a, in, James, cold, winter)

2 Tiffany는 보통 주말에 집에 있다. (the, usually, Tiffany, weekend, on, at, home, is)

3 나의 스마트폰은 가끔 작동을 멈춘다. (smartphone, working, my, stops, sometimes)

4 너는 항상 나의 충고를 기억해야 한다. (my, remember, you, always, advice, must)

5 결정을 한다는 것은 가끔 어렵다. (is, it, decision, to, difficult, make, a, sometimes)

6 그는 보통 지하철을 타고 학교에 간다. (usually, school, he, subway, by, goes, to)

7 나는 인도로의 여행을 절대 잊지 않을 것이다. (forget, the, will, trip, India, never, I, to)

8 진수는 가끔 그의 사진을 보려고 Tom의 블로그를 방문한다.
(Tom's, to, his, Jinsu, sometimes, blog, pictures, see, visits)

9 올해에 태풍들이 제주도에 자주 왔다. (often, Jeju, typhoons, came, this, to, year)

B 보기에서 알맞은 표현을 찾아 우리말에 맞게 영어로 쓰시오.

online
one's customers
give up on
on Mondays
after a meal
an email
should keep

1 Jerry는 가끔씩 나에게 이메일을 보낸다.

____

2 그 점원은 항상 그의 고객들에게 친절하다.

____

3 Susie는 절대 그녀의 꿈을 포기하지 않을 것이다.

____

4 Katie는 종종 온라인으로 옷을 산다.

____

5 Jenny는 보통 월요일에 바쁘다.

____

6 Ron은 가끔 식사 후에 디저트를 먹는다.

____

7 너는 도서관에서 항상 조용히 해야 한다.

____

C 그림을 보고 보기에서 알맞은 표현을 찾아 전자기기 사용 빈도에 대한 문장을 쓰시오.

watch movies	send text messages	read e-books	surf the Internet

0 

(computer)

Sunju usually uses her computer to write on her blog.

She sometimes plays games on it.

1 

(tablet PC)

1) Daeho ______________________________.

2) ______________________________

2 

(smartphone)

1) Sena ______________________________.

2) ______________________________

WRAP UP

A 다음은 할로윈 파티의 모습이다. 괄호 안의 단어와 보기의 표현을 활용하여 그림 속 인물들의 복장을 묘사하는 문장을 쓰시오.

laugh cry dance

0 *The sleeping boy is wearing a ghost costume.* (ghost)

1 ________________ (vampire)

2 ________________ (pumpkin)

3 ________________ (princess)

B 보기에서 알맞은 단어를 찾아 진혁이가 건강을 유지하기 위해 하는 일에 대해 쓰시오.

always sometimes usually never

0 Jinhyuk drinks water eight times a day. *He often drinks water.*

1 Jinhyuk walks to school every morning.

____

2 Jinhyuk doesn't eat fast food at all.

____

3 Jinhyuk plays tennis twice a week.

____

4 Jinhyuk goes to bed early almost every day.

____

C 다음 우리말에 맞게 영어로 쓰시오.

1

그 불타는 건물은 매우 위험해 보였다. (burn)

2

Amy는 때때로 시험에서 실수들을 한다. (make mistakes)

3

나의 삼촌은 작년에 중고차를 구입하셨다. (use)

4

나는 지금부터 절대 컴퓨터 게임을 하지 않을 것이다. (from now on)

5

Matt는 영화를 제작하는 것에 관심이 있다. (make films)

6

Julie는 자주 Bob과 점심을 먹는다.

7

내 점수는 매우 만족스러웠다. (grades)

D 다음 우리말에 맞게 영어로 쓰시오.

1

Yesterday was Dan's birthday. Sam and I prepared a surprise party and presents for him. Sam gave him a nice cap. 1) 나는 그에게 흥미진진한 소설을 주었다. Dan liked our presents. 2) 그는 매우 감동한 것처럼 보였다.

1)

2) (touch)

2

Joe's Kitchen is my favorite restaurant. 1) 나의 가족은 종종 그 레스토랑에 간다. I usually order the steak because it is very good. You should try it too. 2) 그것은 절대 당신을 실망시키지 않을 것이다.

1)

2) (never)

E 주어진 정보를 바탕으로 책에 대한 감상문을 쓰시오.

0 ★★★★★

Love Me (love, touch, sad)

The love story was very touching.

I was touched by the sad story.

1 ★★★★★

Detective Hong (detective, thrill, scary)

1) ....

2) ....

2 ★★★★★

The Space (sci-fi, bore, simple)

1) ....

2) ....

F 주어진 정보를 바탕으로 펜팔에게 자신의 취미생활을 소개하는 이메일을 쓰시오.

- play basketball after school (usually)
- have a basketball game on Sunday morning (sometimes)
- win the game (always), interesting

Hi Patrick,

I will tell you about my favorite hobby. My hobby is playing basketball.

1 ....

2 ....

3 ....

Seho

LESSON 10

비교

UNIT 1 원급, 비교급, 최상급
UNIT 2 원급, 비교급을 이용한 최상급 표현

paint	state	rating	feather
expensive	place	long jumper	wool
sweet	Antarctica	far	fashionable
cheap	country	weightlifter	soft
popular	subject	comfortable	silk
dish	history	diligent	convenient
product	material	comedian	unhealthy
weight	hard	joke	offer
light	price	bus stop	option
bridge	service	again	dirty

UNIT 1 원급, 비교급, 최상급

I shoot **better than** boys.

1 '~만큼 …한[하게]'라는 의미로 정도가 동등한 둘을 비교할 때 〈as + 원급 + as〉를 쓴다.

Tomorrow will be **as cold as** today.

Julie paints **as well as** her sister.

2 '~보다 더 …한[하게]'라는 의미로 두 개의 대상을 비교할 때 〈비교급 + than〉을 쓴다.

Women usually live **longer than** men.

Sam likes soccer **more than** baseball.

3 '가장 ~한[하게]'라는 의미로 세 가지 이상을 비교하여 정도가 가장 높은 것을 표현할 때 〈the + 최상급〉을 쓴다.

This is **the most expensive** bag in the store.

I like this jacket **the best** of the three.

Note

〈one of the + 최상급 + 복수명사〉는 '가장 ~한 것들 중의 하나'라는 의미이다.

Messi is **one of the best soccer players** in the world.

A 괄호 안의 표현을 활용하여 우리말에 맞게 영어로 쓰시오.

1 이 햄스터는 내 손만큼 작다. (this hamster, small, my hand)

2 8월은 한 해 중 가장 더운 달이다. (August, hot, month, the year)

3 이 연극은 그 책보다 더 흥미진진하다. (this play, exciting, the book)

4 수민이의 방은 그녀의 언니 것만큼 크다. (Sumin's room, big, her sister's)

5 주스를 마시는 것이 콜라를 마시는 것보다 더 낫다.
(drinking juice, good, drinking Coke)

6 추석은 한국에서 가장 큰 명절들 중 하나이다. (Chuseok, big, holiday, Korea)

B 보기에서 알맞은 표현을 찾아 우리말에 맞게 영어로 쓰시오.

cell phone
yours
dancing
the USA
a lemon
dishes

1 Jane의 컴퓨터는 너의 것만큼 오래되었다.

....

2 오렌지는 레몬보다 더 달다.

....

3 나는 그 가게에서 가장 싼 휴대전화를 샀다.

....

4 미국에서 농구는 야구만큼 인기가 있다.

....

5 나는 춤추는 것보다 노래하는 것을 더 좋아한다.

....

6 피자는 세계에서 가장 인기 있는 요리들 중 하나이다.

....

C 다음 표에 주어진 정보를 바탕으로 세 노트북을 비교하는 문장을 쓰시오.

Product	Ultra laptop	Ocean laptop	Air laptop
Weight	1.3 kg	1.6 kg	1.6 kg
Battery Life	3 hours	2 hours	3 hours
Size	14 inch	14 inch	15 inch

0 Ultra laptop

The Ultra laptop is the lightest of the three. <Weight / three>

The Ultra laptop's battery life is as long as the Air laptop's. <Battery Life / Air laptop>

1 Ocean laptop

1) .... <Size / Air laptop>

2) .... <Battery Life / three>

2 Air laptop

1) .... <Weight / Ocean laptop>

2) .... <Size / three>

UNIT 2 원급, 비교급을 이용한 최상급 표현

I am **prettier than any other girl**, thanks to my red hair.

★ 원급과 비교급을 사용하여 최상급의 의미를 표현할 수 있다. 〈No ~ + as + 원급 + as〉, 〈No ~ + 비교급 + than〉, 〈비교급 + than any other + 단수명사〉는 최상급의 의미이다.

Incheon Bridge is the longest bridge in Korea.

→ **No** bridge in Korea is **as long as** Incheon Bridge.

→ **No** bridge in Korea is **longer than** Incheon Bridge.

→ Incheon Bridge is **longer than any other bridge** in Korea.

A 괄호 안의 단어를 배열하여 올바른 문장으로 다시 쓰시오.

1 알래스카는 미국에 있는 다른 어떤 주보다 크다.
(than, in, bigger, Alaska, the USA, is, other, state, any)

2 어떤 동물도 사람보다 똑똑하지 않다. (smarter, animal, than, man, no, is)

3 우리 동아리에 있는 어떤 선수도 Amanda만큼 어리지 않다.
(young, Amanda, player, our, is, club, in, as, no, as)

4 Joe는 그의 반에 있는 다른 어떤 학생보다 키가 크다.
(class, than, taller, other, Joe, his, any, is, student, in)

5 세계에 어떤 곳도 남극보다 춥지 않다.
(world, is, no, Antarctica, colder, place, in, the, than)

6 중국에서 어떤 가수도 그녀만큼 인기가 있지 않다.
(singer, in, as, popular, no, is, her, as, China)

7 Carlos는 그의 나라에서 다른 어떤 사람보다 부유하다.
(Carlos, man, than, his, country, is, other, in, richer, any)

B 보기에서 알맞은 단어를 찾아 우리말에 맞게 영어로 쓰시오.

보기
building
Russia
dish
vitamin C
material
girl
history
coat

1 세계에 어떤 나라도 러시아보다 크지 않다.

2 어떤 과목도 역사만큼 재미있지 않다.

3 키위는 다른 어떤 과일보다 비타민 C를 많이 가지고 있다.

4 우리 반에 있는 어떤 소녀도 Maria보다 빠르지 않다.

5 이 도시의 어떤 건물도 이 학교만큼 오래되지 않았다.

6 이것이 이 가게에서 다른 어떤 코트보다 더 가볍다.

7 이 식당에 있는 어떤 음식도 스테이크만큼 비싸지 않다.

8 세계에 어떤 물질도 다이아몬드보다 더 단단하지 않다.

C 주어진 단어를 활용하여 다음과 같이 비교하는 문장을 쓰시오.

0
- old
- Bongjeongsa
- Hagar Qim

Bongjeongsa is older than any other building in Korea.

No building in the world is older than Hagar Qim.

1
- tall
- Mt. Baekdu
- Mt. Everest

1)

2)

2
- long
- the Nakdong River
- the Nile River

1)

2)

WRAP UP

A 주어진 정보를 바탕으로 세 호텔을 비교하는 문장을 쓰시오.

Grand Hotel	Sunbeach Hotel	Oxford Hotel
Built in 2002	Built in 1978	Built in 2002
Service Rating: ★★★	Service Rating: ★★★★	Service Rating: ★★★★★
Room Price: $ 200	Room Price: $ 130	Room Price: $ 130

1 Sunbeach Hotel ______________________ Oxford Hotel. <price>

2 Sunbeach Hotel ______________________ Grand Hotel. <service>

3 Oxford Hotel ______________________ Grand Hotel. <age>

4 Grand Hotel ______________________ Sunbeach Hotel. <price>

5 Grand Hotel ______________________ the three. <service>

B 괄호 안의 단어를 활용하여 세계 최고의 운동 선수에 대한 문장을 쓰시오.

0 Taehwan (swimmer, swim, fast)

No swimmer in the world swam faster than Taehwan. <비교급 + than>

1 Mike (long jumper, jump, far)

______________________ <as + 원급 + as>

2 Yuna (figure skater, be, good)

______________________ <비교급 + than>

3 Usain (runner, run, fast)

______________________ <as + 원급 + as>

4 Miran (weightlifter, lift, a heavy weight)

______________________ <비교급 + than any other>

C 다음 우리말에 맞게 영어로 쓰시오.

1

어떤 곳도 나의 집만큼 편하지 않다.

2

Michael Jackson은 세계에서 최고의 가수들 중 한 명이었다.

3

그 영화는 그 책보다 더 재미있었다.

4

Max는 세 명의 형제들 중에서 가장 어리다.

5

우리 팀에 있는 어떤 선수도 Jordan만큼 잘하지 못한다. (on one's team)

6

John은 나의 반에 있는 다른 어떤 학생보다 부지런하다. (diligent)

7

어떤 꽃도 사람보다 더 아름답지 않다. (beautiful, man)

D 다음 우리말에 맞게 영어로 쓰시오.

1

> 1) Steve는 우리 반에서 가장 인기가 있는 소년이다. He is very kind to everyone. Also, 2) 그는 코미디언만큼 웃긴다. All his classmates laugh at his jokes. He makes us happy all the time.

1) ____________________

2) ____________________ (comedian)

2

> This morning, I saw a girl at the bus stop. 1) 그녀는 꽃보다 더 아름다웠다. 2) 세상에 어떤 소녀도 그녀보다 예쁘지 않다. I want to see her again tomorrow.

1) ____________________

2) ____________________

E 주어진 정보를 바탕으로 패션 소품에 관한 광고문을 쓰시오.

0 (light, a feather / comfortable)

You will feel that these shoes are as light as a feather.
No shoes are more comfortable than these!

1 (warm, wool / fashionable)

1) ______________________________

2) ______________________________

2 (soft, a silk / beautiful)

1) ______________________________

2) ______________________________

F 보기에서 외식의 장점과 단점에 해당하는 단어를 한 개씩 골라 그 장점과 단점에 대한 문장을 쓰시오.

convenient	expensive	quick	unhealthy

Advantages

0 *Eating out usually offers more food options than eating at home.*

1 ______________________________

Disadvantages

0 *Eating out is usually dirtier than eating at home.*

2 ______________________________

LESSON 11

대명사

UNIT 1 부정대명사 some, any, one
UNIT 2 부정대명사 all, both, each, every, no

wrong	art	refrigerator	unique
idea	sketchbook	snowboard	come with
useful	gym	wind-surf	piece
toilet	own	language	provide
bathroom	be allowed to	price tag	refill
borrow	clothes	on sale	item
join	get together	on time	for free
topic	fit	bakery	personal
doughnut	locker	off	trainer
grammar	talent	character	exchange

UNIT 1 부정대명사 some, any, one

I don't need **any** recipes when I cook.

★ 막연한 사람이나 사물을 가리키는 대명사를 부정대명사라고 한다.

1 '약간(의), 몇몇(의)'라는 의미를 나타낼 때 some 또는 any를 쓴다. some은 보통 긍정문이나 권유문에, any는 보통 부정문이나 의문문에 쓴다.
Some of my answers are wrong. Would you like **some** tea?
Susan wanted to buy **some** kiwis, but they didn't have **any**.
I don't have **any** plans for this weekend.
Do you have **any** ideas?

2 앞에 언급된 명사와 같은 종류의 사물을 나타낼 때 one을 쓰며, 복수형은 ones이다.
Jennifer lost her smartphone, so she needs to buy **one**.
Old shoes are more comfortable than new **ones**.

Note

1 some과 any는 형용사처럼 명사 앞에 쓰이기도 한다.

2 앞에 언급된 것과 동일한 것을 나타낼 때는 it을 쓴다.
I lost my smartphone, but I found it.

A

괄호 안의 표현과 some, any, one(s), it 중 하나를 활용하여 우리말에 맞게 영어로 쓰시오.

1 나의 선생님께서 나에게 몇 가지 유용한 충고를 해주셨다. (give, me, useful advice)

2 화장실에 휴지가 없다. (there, toilet paper, in the bathroom)

3 이 오렌지들은 너무 작아서 나는 더 큰 것들을 원한다. (too small, so, want, bigger)

4 나는 내 열쇠를 찾아봤지만, 그것을 찾을 수 없었다. (look for, can't find)

5 요즘 재미있는 영화가 있니? (there, interesting movies, these days)

6 초콜릿 케이크를 조금 더 드시겠어요? (would you like, more chocolate cake)

7 나는 내 펜들을 가져 오는 것을 잊었지만 하나 빌릴 수 있었다. (forget to bring, can borrow)

B 보기에서 알맞은 표현을 찾아 우리말에 맞게 영어로 쓰시오.

doughnuts
at home
a soccer club
homework
the topic
too old
more than

1 Sue는 지난 일요일에 집에서 몇 편의 영화를 봤다.

2 내 컴퓨터는 너무 오래되어서 나는 새 것을 사고 싶다.

3 내 친구들 중 몇 명은 축구 동아리에 가입했다.

4 그 주제에 관한 질문이 좀 있나요?

5 도넛 좀 드시겠어요?

6 Karen은 새 것들보다 옛날 노래들을 듣는 것을 더 좋아한다.

7 Maria는 어제 숙제가 없었다.

C 사진을 보고 사고 싶어하는 물품에 대한 문장을 쓰시오.

0 

- grammar book

Mary needs to study English grammar.

But she doesn't have any grammar books.

She wants to buy one.

1 

- sketchbook

Henry needs to draw a picture in art class.

1)

2)

2 

- gym shoes

Mina needs to exercise.

1)

2)

UNIT 2 부정대명사 all, both, each, every, no

*I dress in **both** pants and dresses.*
*They **all** look good together.*

1 all: 모두, 모든

All (of) the questions on the test were difficult.

2 both: 둘 다, 양쪽(의)

Both (of) my parents are dentists.

3 each: 각각(의)

Each country has its own flag.

Each of them has their own dream.

4 every: 모든

Every student in this school knows the teacher.

5 no: 어떤 ~도 (아닌)

No pets are allowed to enter this market.

Note

1 all, both, each는 대명사뿐만 아니라 형용사처럼 명사 앞에 쓰이기도 하지만 every와 no는 항상 명사 앞에만 쓰인다.

2 보통 뒤에 명사가 오는 경우 그 명사의 수에 따라 동사를 쓰지만, each와 every는 뒤에 단수명사와 단수동사를 쓴다.

A 그림을 보고 각 보기에서 알맞은 표현을 찾아 문장을 쓰시오. (단, 모두 현재형으로 쓰시오.)

1 

2 

3 

4 

All the people in my family No clothes in this store Every student in this school Each person	order a different dish get together on New Year's Day fit me have a locker

1 ______________________________

2 ______________________________

3 ______________________________

4 ______________________________

B 보기에서 알맞은 표현을 찾아 우리말에 맞게 영어로 쓰시오.

get an A
in the refrigerator
one's math teacher
one's own hobby
do one's best
Korean food
a different talent

1 우리 반의 모든 학생들은 우리 수학 선생님을 좋아한다.

....

2 각각의 사람은 다른 재능을 가지고 있다.

....

3 Patrick은 모든 과목에서 A를 받았다.

....

4 내 미국인 친구들 둘 다 한국 음식을 좋아한다.

....

5 냉장고 안에 우유가 없다.

....

6 모든 선수들은 경기에서 최선을 다했다.

....

7 우리 각자는 우리만의 취미를 가지고 있다.

....

C 주어진 표현을 활용하여 친구들이 계절별로 좋아하는 야외활동에 대해 쓰시오.

0
- snowboard
- winter
- a snowboard

Jonghyun and Andy *go snowboarding every winter*.

Both like snowboarding a lot.

Each of them has a snowboard.

1
- wind-surf
- summer
- a surfboard

1) Subin and Ron ....

2) ....

3) ....

2
- mountain bike
- fall
- a mountain bike

1) Minsu and Katie ....

2) ....

3) ....

WRAP UP

A

그림을 보고 각 보기에서 알맞은 표현을 찾아 다음 그림을 묘사한 문장을 쓰시오.

0 

1 

2 

3 

each both any

a different language soccer player money

0 Maria bought some cookies. She gave me one.

1 Julie has two brothers. ______________________

2 Jeongmi lost her purse this morning. ______________________

3 Three people are from three different countries.

____

B

보기의 단어와 괄호 안의 표현을 활용하여 인형가게를 묘사한 문장을 쓰시오.

no some each

0 All the teddy bears in the store are cute. (be cute)

1 ______________________ (have a price tag)

2 ______________________ (be on sale)

3 ______________________ (be wearing shoes)

C 다음 우리말에 맞게 영어로 쓰시오.

1

Jessica는 모든 문제를 제시간에 풀었다. (on time)

2

Sara는 토요일에 수업이 없다. (classes)

3

각각의 학교는 그곳만의 교가를 가지고 있다. (school song)

4

Mike는 그의 오래된 카메라를 팔고, 그는 새 것을 샀다.

5

우리 둘 다 점심으로 스테이크를 주문했다.

6

이 식당에서 모든 음식은 맛있다.

7

James는 제과점에서 조금의 빵을 샀다. (bakery)

D 다음 우리말에 맞게 영어로 쓰시오.

1

The department store was having a sale, so Amy went shopping to buy a T-shirt. 1) 모든 티셔츠가 30%~50% 할인을 했다. But 2) 그녀는 멋진 티셔츠를 찾을 수 없었다. She didn't buy any, and she was disappointed.

1) ________________ (30%~50% off)

2) ________________

2

My favorite movie is *Harry Potter*. I watched all the movies in the *Harry Potter* series. 1) 각 영화는 다른 이야기를 가지고 있다. 2) 모든 등장인물은 독특하고 재미있다. I love them.

1) ________________

2) ________________ (character, unique)

E 주어진 정보를 바탕으로 각 상점의 이벤트에 관한 글을 쓰시오.

0 Heaven Coffee Shop Grand Opening!

- cup of coffee, come with, a piece of cake
- a free refill, for, cup of coffee

Every cup of coffee comes with a piece of cake.
We provide a free refill for each cup of coffee.

1 Cara Clothing Store Grand Opening!

- item, be, on sale
- 30 percent off, on, item

1) ______________________

2) ______________________

2 ACE Fitness Center Grand Opening!

- member, use, a locker for free
- a personal trainer, for, member

1) ______________________

2) ______________________

F 주어진 표현과 보기의 단어를 활용하여 그림 1, 2, 3 이 나타내는 상황을 각각 묘사하는 문장을 쓰시오.

1

- order

2

- big for me

3

- exchange ~ for, smaller

ones	some	all

1 I ______________________ online.

2 ______________________

3 ______________________

LESSON 12

자주 쓰이는 표현

UNIT 1 가목적어 it
UNIT 2 동사 get의 쓰임

nail	impossible	hit	turn down
necessary	ahead	medicine	burn
enjoyable	stay up	stain	remove
mall	take notes	jam	pimple
fight	cheat	repairman	upset
index	bite	vet	annoyed
consider	mosquito	treat	in front of
volunteer	perm	apologize	inside
make noise	refund	pull out	stadium
regularly	information	deliver	crowd

UNIT 1 가목적어 it

*I think **it** strange to eat nails in a soup.*

★ 목적어로 쓰인 to부정사구가 긴 경우, 목적어 자리에 가목적어 it을 쓰고 to부정사구는 문장 뒤로 보낸다.

Jay found **it** necessary *to practice writing English a lot*.

Dan thought **it** important *to have a true friend*.

Smartphones make **it** easier *to surf the Internet*.

A 괄호 안의 단어를 배열하여 올바른 문장으로 다시 쓰시오.

1 Mary는 테니스 치는 것이 즐겁다고 생각한다.
(play, Mary, enjoyable, it, to, thinks, tennis)

....

2 나는 쇼핑몰에서 시간을 보내는 것이 재미있다는 것을 알았다.
(it, spend, time, mall, found, to, fun, the, I, at)

....

3 Jessica는 친구들과 싸우는 것이 잘못되었다고 느꼈다.
(it, to, felt, fight, friends, with, Jessica, wrong)

....

4 그 색인은 그 단어들을 찾는 것을 쉽게 해주었다.
(to, the, find, index, it, made, easy, words, the)

....

5 Max는 자원봉사를 하는 것이 중요하다고 여긴다.
(considers, Max, do, to, volunteer work, it, important)

....

6 우리는 영어로 이메일 쓰기가 어렵다는 것을 알았다.
(found, it, write, email, we, difficult, in, to, English, an)

....

7 사람들은 미술관에서 떠드는 것이 무례하다고 생각한다.
(rude, a, think, noise, make, gallery, people, it, to, in,)

....

B **보기에서 알맞은 표현을 찾아 우리말에 맞게 영어로 쓰시오.**

help poor children
exercise regularly
find the restaurant
arrive on time
wear a helmet
learn Korean
break the rules

1 Eddie는 헬멧을 쓰는 것이 중요하다고 생각한다.

2 Jessi는 한국어를 배우는 것이 재미있다는 것을 알았다.

3 Nancy는 가난한 아이들을 돕는 것이 필요하다고 느꼈다.

4 그 표지판들은 그 식당을 찾는 것을 쉽게 해준다.

5 사람들은 규칙적으로 운동하는 것이 중요하다고 여긴다.

6 Ron은 규칙들을 어기는 것이 잘못되었다고 생각한다.

7 나는 제시간에 도착하는 것이 불가능하다는 것을 알았다.

C **그림을 보고 보기에서 알맞은 표현을 찾아 좋은 성적을 위해 해야 할 것과 하지 말아야 할 것에 대해 쓰시오.**

read the questions carefully   take notes   sleep during class   cheat on the exam

0 

I found it important to plan ahead.

I found it wrong to stay up all night.

1 

1)

2)

2 

1)

2)

UNIT 2 동사 get의 쓰임

She needs to **get** her clothes **cleaned**.

1 〈get + 목적어〉에서 get은 보통 '~을 얻다, 받다'라는 의미이다.

I **got** my report card yesterday.

Tony **got** an email from his old friend.

2 〈get + 보어〉에서 get은 보통 '~한 상태가 되다'라는 의미이다.

It is **getting cold**.

After Julie drank the milk, she **got sick**.

3 〈get + 목적어 + to-v〉에서 get은 '~을 …하게 시키다'라는 의미이다.

My brother **got** me **to clean** his room.

Mike's sister always **gets** him **to cook** ramen.

4 〈get + v-ed〉나 〈get + 목적어 + v-ed〉에서 get은 '(주어나 목적어)가 어떤 일을 당하다'라는 의미이다.

Aiden **got bitten** by a mosquito.

Sean **got** his hair **permed** yesterday.

A **괄호 안의 표현과 get을 활용하여 우리말에 맞게 영어로 쓰시오.**

1 Lily는 그 셔츠에 대한 환불을 받았다. (a refund for)

2 Serena는 어제 그녀의 손톱을 칠했다. (her nails, paint)

3 Karen는 그 일이 지겨워졌다. (bore with)

4 나는 그 영화를 보고 난 후 슬퍼졌다. (after, watch the movie, sad)

5 Julie는 종종 생일파티에 초대된다. (invite, to the birthday parties)

6 나의 아빠는 우리 개에게 신문을 가져오게 하신다. (bring the newspaper)

7 우리는 인터넷에서 많은 정보를 얻을 수 있다. (information, on the Internet)

8 Henry의 여자친구는 그가 운동을 시작하게 했다. (start exercising)

B 보기에서 알맞은 표현을 찾아 우리말에 맞게 영어로 쓰시오.

do dishes better wash dark finish a Christmas card hit by a bicycle

1 요즘은 오후 6시에 어두워진다.

2 Joe는 그의 조부모에게서 크리스마스 카드를 받았다.

3 내 고양이가 어제 자전거에 치였다.

4 Tom은 그의 아버지의 자동차를 세차했다.

5 Mary는 그녀의 여동생에게 설거지를 하게 했다.

6 당신이 이 약을 복용하면 곧 더 나아질 것입니다.

7 우리는 우리의 숙제를 제시간에 끝마쳤다.

C 괄호 안의 표현을 활용하여 그림을 묘사하는 문장을 쓰시오.

0 

(shirt, stain / the cleaner, clean)

My shirt got stained.

So I got the cleaner to clean it.

1 

(printer, jam / the repairman, fix)

1)

2)

2 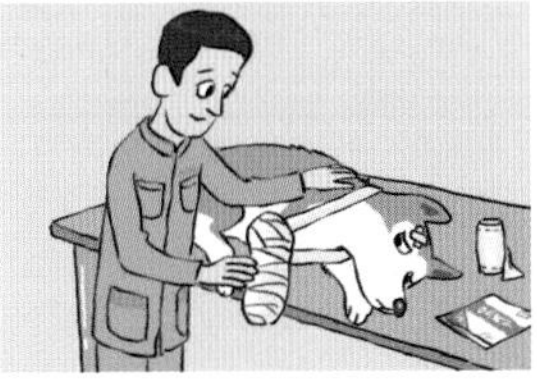

(dog, hurt / the vet, treat)

1)

2)

WRAP UP

A 보기에서 알맞은 표현을 찾아 각 문제에 대한 해결책을 쓰시오.

buy a new one	visit an eye doctor
wear a scarf	apologize first

0 George got a bad score on the midterm exam.

He thought it wise to take online classes.

1 Sera had a sore throat.

2 Juhyun had trouble seeing the whiteboard.

3 Dongkyu's alarm clock got broken.

4 Jenny fought with her friend.

B 그림을 보고 보기에서 알맞은 단어를 찾아 수진이가 지난 주말에 한 일에 대해 쓰시오.

0 

1 

2 

3 

repair	pull out	deliver

Sujin was very busy last weekend.

0 *She got the tire changed.*

1

2

3

C 다음 우리말에 맞게 영어로 쓰시오.

1

나는 나의 오빠에게 나의 가방들을 들게 했다. (carry)

2

Eva는 애완동물을 키우는 것이 어렵다는 것을 알았다. (keep pets)

3

그 남자는 그의 차를 수리하게 했다. (repair)

4

Sue는 그녀의 생일에 많은 선물을 받았다. (present)

5

나는 그 사실을 말하는 것이 옳다고 생각했다. (truth)

6

Ted는 그의 남동생에게 볼륨을 줄이게 했다. (turn down)

7

어떤 학생들은 아침에 공부하는 것이 더 낫다고 느낀다.

D 다음 우리말에 맞게 영어로 쓰시오.

1

I went to a beach with my friends yesterday. I enjoyed swimming, but I forgot to use sunscreen. 1) 내 피부가 심하게 탔다. So, it hurt. 2) 나는 선크림을 사용하는 것이 필요하다는 것을 알았다.

1) ______________________________ (badly)

2) ______________________________ (necessary)

2

Our class was going to attend the English play contest. 1) 우리 영어 선생님은 매일 우리가 연극 연습을 하게 하셨다. At first, we were not good. However, we did our best and 2) 우리는 더 나아졌다. At last, we got first prize in the English play contest.

1) ______________________________

2) ______________________________

E

주어진 정보를 바탕으로 구입한 상품의 후기를 쓰시오.

0

Miracle Lotion

- remove pimples
- bad, upset

Recommend ☐ Not recommend ☑

They said that this lotion makes it easy to remove pimples.

But my skin got worse because of it, and I got upset.

1

Zero Drink

- lose weight
- fat, angry

Recommend ☐ Not recommend ☑

1) ______________________

2) ______________________

2

Window Spray

- wash windows
- dirty, annoyed

Recommend ☐ Not recommend ☑

1) ______________________

2) ______________________

F

각 보기에서 운동 경기를 경기장에서 관람하는 것의 장점과 단점에 해당하는 표현을 한 개씩 골라 그 장점과 단점에 대한 문장을 쓰시오.

annoying fun exciting expensive

watch the game right in front of you
cheer with other fans
buy snacks inside the stadium
walk through the crowds

Advantages

0 You will find it enjoyable to meet your favorite players before the game.

1 ______________________

Disadvantages

0 You will find it uncomfortable to sit for hours during the game.

2 ______________________

SECTION 3

PATTERNS FOR WRITING

Useful Patterns for Writing 1

★ be curious about ~: ~에 대해 궁금해하다
I **am curious about** your hobby.

★ be aware of ~: ~을 알고 있다
I **am aware of** his opinion.

1 그 아이들은 그 작은 동물에 대해 궁금해했다. (kid)

2 Rosa는 그녀의 문제에 대해 알고 있었다.

3 나는 하늘에 있는 별들이 궁금하다.

4 David는 내 나쁜 습관들을 알고 있다.

5 그는 우리의 새로운 계획에 대해 궁금해했다.

6 우리는 우리의 상황을 알고 있다. (situation)

7 사람들은 그의 새 책에 대해 궁금해한다.

8 Jane은 그 중요한 사실을 알고 있다. (fact)

9 Sally는 그 잘생긴 배우가 궁금했었다.

10 그들은 학교 규칙들에 대해 알고 있다. (rule)

Useful Patterns *for Writing* 2

★ agree[disagree, don't agree] with ~: ~에 동의한다[동의하지 않는다]
I **agree with** your opinion.
James **disagrees[doesn't agree with]** his sister's idea.

★ be against ~: ~에 대해 반대한다
I **am against** the law.

1 나는 내 여동생에게 동의하지 않는다.

2 나는 네 계획에 반대한다.

3 나는 Sam의 제안에 동의했다. (suggestion)

4 그들은 그 규칙들에 반대한다. (rule)

5 Tom은 그의 아내에게 동의할 것이다.

6 우리는 이 전쟁에 반대한다.

7 그녀는 내 결정에 동의하지 않았다. (decision)

8 Amy는 그 해결책에 반대했다. (solution)

9 Susan은 John의 주장에 동의했다. (argument)

10 우리는 그 새로운 정책에 반대한다. (policy)

Useful Patterns for Writing 3

★ don't think that ~: ~라고 생각하지 않는다

I **don't think that** he is honest.

★ suggest[recommend] that ~: ~을 제안하다[권하다]

I **suggest that** we (should) plant trees here.

She **recommended that** I (should) eat more vegetables.

1 나는 Lily가 친절하다고 생각하지 않는다.

2 나는 당신이 이 액션 영화를 볼 것을 제안합니다.

3 나는 이 시계가 싸다고 생각하지 않는다.

4 의사들은 우리가 많은 물을 마시는 것을 권한다.

5 나는 내일 비가 올 거라고 생각하지 않는다.

6 그는 우리가 일찍 집을 떠날 것을 제안했다.

7 나는 Emma가 좋은 가수라고 생각하지 않는다.

8 그녀는 내가 그 박물관을 방문할 것을 권했다.

9 나는 돈이 아주 중요하다고 생각하지 않는다.

10 Jenny는 우리가 제주도로 여행가는 것을 제안했다. (travel, Jejudo)

Useful Patterns for Writing 4

★ seem[appear] to-v: ~인 것 같다
He **seems to be** sick.

★ be worried about ~: ~에 대해 걱정한다
I **am worried about** the final exam.

1 Sally가 너를 좋아하는 것 같다.

2 나는 내 시험 결과가 걱정된다. (test results)

3 그는 매우 피곤한 것 같았다.

4 Nick은 그의 딸의 건강에 대해 걱정한다.

5 너는 많은 친구를 가지고 있는 것 같다.

6 나는 그의 건강에 해로운 식습관이 걱정된다. (unhealthy diet)

7 그녀는 수영하는 것을 즐기는 것 같았다.

8 Julie는 그녀의 발표에 대해 걱정했다. (presentation)

9 그는 내 이야기를 믿는 것 같다.

10 내 부모님은 내 미래에 대해 걱정하신다.

Useful Patterns for Writing 5

★ nearly[completely] forgot about[that] ~: ~에 대해[하다는 것을] 하마터면 잊을뻔했다 [완전히 잊었다]
I **nearly forgot that** I had an appointment.

★ never forget ~: ~을 결코 잊지 않는다
I will **never forget** your kindness.

1 그녀는 회의가 있다는 것을 하마터면 잊을뻔했다.

2 나는 당신의 도움을 결코 잊지 않을 것이다.

3 Ava는 그녀의 약속을 완전히 잊어버렸다.

4 그는 결코 그의 나라를 잊지 않았다.

5 그는 그의 삼촌의 결혼식을 하마터면 잊을뻔했다.

6 나는 내 중학교 친구들을 결코 잊지 않을 것이다.

7 우리는 그가 우리를 기다리고 있었다는 것을 완전히 잊어버렸다. (wait for)

8 그녀는 David의 부드러운 목소리를 결코 잊지 않았다.

9 나는 하마터면 내 영어 숙제에 대해 잊을뻔했다.

10 나는 그 마지막 장면을 결코 잊지 않을 것이다. (scene)

Useful Patterns for Writing 6

★ be allowed to-v: ~하도록 허락되다
He **was allowed to attend** the meeting.

★ be likely to-v: ~할 것 같다
It **is likely to rain** today.

1 당신은 네 권의 책을 대출하는 것이 허용된다. (check out)

2 그녀는 늦게 도착할 것 같다.

3 학생들은 오늘 일찍 집에 가도록 허락되었다.

4 Jack은 그 시험에 통과할 것 같다.

5 우리는 한 시간 동안 TV를 보는 것이 허락되었다.

6 그들은 이 호텔에서 머물 것 같다.

7 방문객들은 이 건물에 들어가는 것이 허락되었다. (enter)

8 Emily는 그 계획을 취소할 것 같다.

9 그들은 여기에서 농구를 하는 것이 허용된다.

10 Rick은 테니스 동아리에 들 것 같다. (club)

Useful Patterns for Writing 7

★ would like to-v: ~하고 싶다
I would like to buy a new smartphone.

★ Would you mind v-ing ~?: ~해주시겠어요?
Would you mind explaining it again?

1 나는 쇼핑하러 가고 싶다.

2 저와 함께 가주시겠어요?

3 나는 세수를 하고 싶다.

4 이 창문을 닫아주시겠어요?

5 나는 햄버거가 먹고 싶다.

6 제게 당신의 자전거를 빌려주시겠어요?

7 저는 내일 당신의 사무실을 방문하고 싶습니다. (office)

8 제 사진을 찍어주시겠어요?

9 저는 과학 선생님이 되고 싶어요.

10 음량을 낮춰주시겠어요? (lower, volume)

Useful Patterns for Writing 8

★ Remember to-v[v-ing]: ~할 것을[했던 것을] 기억해라
Remember to call me tonight.
Remember going to Chicago with me.

★ Don't forget to-v: ~할 것을 잊지 마라
Don't forget to do your homework.

1 교실에 있는 그 컴퓨터를 끄는 걸 기억해라. (turn off)

2 화장실을 청소해야 하는 것을 잊지 마라.

3 나에게 돈을 좀 빌렸던 것을 기억해라.

4 Amy에게 그녀의 전화번호를 묻는 것을 잊지 마라.

5 너의 우산을 가져가는 걸 기억해라.

6 너의 친구들을 초대하는 것을 잊지 마라.

7 그 프로젝트를 위해 함께 일했던 것을 기억해라. (project)

8 우리에게 너의 사진들을 보내는 것을 잊지 마라. (photo)

9 이 책을 내일 반납해야 하는 것을 기억해라.

10 문을 잠그는 것을 잊지 마라.

Useful Patterns for Writing 9

★ be interested in ~: ~에 관심이 있다
I **am interested in** Asian music.

★ don't have any[much] interest in ~: ~에 관심이 전혀 없다[많지 않다]
I **don't have any interest in** art.
I **don't have much interest in** playing the violin.

1 나는 가방들을 만드는 것에 관심이 있다.

2 나는 컴퓨터 게임을 하는 것에 관심이 전혀 없다.

3 그녀는 과학을 공부하는 것에 관심이 없다.

4 Justin은 스포츠에 관심이 많지 않다.

5 우리는 프랑스 음식에 관심이 있다.

6 나는 골프에 관심이 전혀 없다.

7 Grace는 결혼에 관심이 없다. (marriage)

8 우리는 역사에 관심이 많지 않다.

9 Sean은 집을 사는 것에 관심이 있다.

10 Amanda는 차에 관심이 전혀 없다.

Useful Patterns ***for Writing*** *10*

★ think A is better than B: B보다 A가 낫다고 생각하다
I think this shirt is better than that one.

★ as + 원급 + as + 주어 + can: ~가 할 수 있는 한 ~하게
Max drove **as slowly as he could.**

1 그는 내 차가 네 것보다 낫다고 생각한다.

2 나는 그 편지들을 내가 할 수 있는 한 일찍 보냈다.

3 나의 엄마는 물을 마시는 것보다 우유를 마시는 것이 낫다고 생각하신다.

4 Alex는 그가 할 수 있는 한 빨리 걸었다.

5 그는 뛰는 것보다 수영을 하는 것이 낫다고 생각한다.

6 나는 내가 할 수 있는 한 빨리 네게 다시 전화를 할 것이다. (soon)

7 사람들은 그녀의 두 번째 앨범이 첫 번째 것보다 낫다고 생각한다.

8 Lucy는 그녀가 할 수 있는 한 열심히 일을 하고 있다.

9 나는 책들을 읽는 것보다 경험하는 것이 낫다고 생각한다. (experience)

10 Sam은 그가 할 수 있는 한 크게 말했다. (loud)

Useful Patterns for Writing 11

★ All you have to do is + 동사원형 ~: 당신은 ~하기만 하면 된다
All you have to do is wait for him.

★ the + 비교급, the + 비교급: ~하면 할수록 더 …하다
The more I eat the ice cream, **the more** I like it.

1 당신은 여기에 사인만 하면 된다.

2 그는 많이 가지면 가질수록 더 원한다.

3 너는 공부를 더 열심히 하기만 하면 된다.

4 나는 나이가 들수록 피곤함을 더 느낀다. (get)

5 너는 조용히 하기만 하면 된다.

6 Andrew는 인도에 오래 머물수록 그 나라가 더 좋아졌다.

7 너는 이 경기에서 이기기만 하면 된다.

8 당신이 이 운동을 많이 하면 할수록 당신은 더 건강해질 것이다.

9 당신은 눈을 감기만 하면 된다.

10 내가 더 높이 올라갈수록 공기는 더 차가워졌다. (go up)

Useful Patterns for Writing 12

★ be supposed to-v: ~해야 한다
We **are supposed to meet** at the café.

★ look forward to + v-ing: ~하기를 고대하다
I am **looking forward to seeing** my favorite singer.

1 당신은 이 상자를 열어서는 안 된다.

2 Patrick은 당신과 함께 일하기를 고대한다.

3 우리는 오늘 우리 집을 페인트칠해야 한다.

4 우리는 그녀의 새 영화를 보기를 고대하고 있다.

5 나는 지난주에 떠나야 했다.

6 나는 여기에서 새로운 친구들을 사귀기를 고대한다. (make friends)

7 우리는 이 빌딩에서 담배를 피워서는 안 된다.

8 Mary는 당신과 다시 이야기를 나누길 고대하고 있다.

9 당신은 여기에 주차해서는 안 된다.

10 우리는 다음 주에 캠핑 가는 것을 고대하고 있다.

WORD LIST

LESSON 1

actress 여배우
comfortable 편안한
soft 부드러운
classroom 교실
invent 발명하다
—
invite 초대하다
famous 유명한
professor 교수
festival 축제
delicious 맛있는
—
seem ~인 것 같다
medicine 약
bitter 쓴
prepare 준비하다
sweet (소리가) 듣기 좋은
—
performance 공연, 연주회
secret 비밀
lawyer 변호사
expect 기대하다
athlete 운동 선수
—
text message 문자 메시지
useful 유용한
director 감독
advise 충고하다
report card 성적표
—
angry 화난
nervous 불안한, 초조한
spicy 매운
hard 열심히
exercise 운동하다
—
angel 천사
cooler 아이스박스
fresh 신선한
bring 가져가다
dizzy 어지러운
—
rest 휴식
touching 감동적인
fun 재미있는
serious 심각한
moving 가슴을 뭉클하게 하는
—
bowl 그릇
salty 짠, 짭짤한

LESSON 2

roof 지붕
trouble 문제
shake 흔들리다
P.E. 체육 (physical education)
magic 마술
—
bark (개 등이) 짖다
cross 건너다
rise 오르다, 올라가다
touch 만지다
clothes 옷
—
essay 에세이
earring 귀걸이
slim 날씬한
hang 매달리다
subway 지하철
—
hospital 병원
plant 식물
hose 호스
stay 머무르다
on time 정각에
—
check 확인하다
sunset 해질녘, 일몰
take a shower 샤워를 하다
arrive 도착하다
cartoon 만화
—
character 등장인물
shoulder 어깨
scream 비명을 지르다
haunted house 유령의 집
parade 퍼레이드, 가두 행진
—
gym 체육관
coach 코치
pass (공을) 패스하다
credit card 신용카드
ship 배, 선박
—
make fun of ~을 놀리다
enter 들어가다
fight 싸우다
on foot 걸어서, 도보로
ride 타다
—
cherry blossoms 벚꽃

playground 운동장
draw 그리다
base (야구) 베이스
bring 가져오다

LESSON 3

turn off (전기 · 가스 등을) 끄다
heater 난방기, 히터
careful 조심하는
wipe 닦다, 훔치다
warm up 준비 운동을 하다
—
asleep 잠이 든
take care of 돌보다
Europe 유럽
graduate 졸업하다
angry 화난
—
lie 거짓말
all day 온종일
mine 나의 것
traffic jam 교통 체증
grade 성적
—
amusement park 놀이 공원
turn on (전기 · 가스 · 수도 등을) 켜다
attend 참석하다
catch a cold 감기 들다
wallet 지갑
—
imagine 상상하다
prize 상, 포상
smart 똑똑한
shop 쇼핑을 하다
online 온라인으로
—
material 자료, 재료
take notes 메모하다
experience 경험
information 정보
enjoyment 즐거움, 기쁨
—
magazine 잡지
get better 좋아지다, 호전되다
soon 곧, 머지않아
uncomfortable 불편한
tight 꽉 조이는
—
practical 실용적인, 유용한

useful 유용한, 도움이 되는
skip 거르다, 빼먹다
focus on 집중하다

LESSON 4

prepare 준비하다
model 모형
gym 체육관
fur 털
hairdresser 미용사
—
pants 바지
pocket 주머니
remote control 리모컨
sofa 소파
monitor 모니터
—
screen 화면
thief 도둑
run away 도망치다
steal 훔치다
baker 제빵사
—
sweet 달콤한, 단
strawberry 딸기
speaker 연설가
hope 희망
writer 작가
—
joy 즐거움
donate 기부하다
poor 가난한
laptop 노트북
receive 받다
—
order 주문하다
travel 여행하다
respect 존경하다
look for 찾다
cartoon 만화
—
hiking trail 하이킹 코스
recommend 추천하다
traditional 전통적인
area 지역
temple 절
—
sommelier 소믈리에
provide 제공하다

service 서비스
barista 바리스타
curator 큐레이터(박물관의 전시 책임자)
—
take care of ~에 대한 책임이 있다
artwork 미술작품
museum 박물관
error 오류
support 지지하다
—
ride 타다; 놀이기구
spicy 매운
kick 차다
wear 입다

LESSON 5

jungle 정글
holiday 휴일
report 보고서
carry 옮기다
take a class 강의를 수강하다
—
fine 좋은
on time 제시간에
memorize 암기하다
sale 할인
department store 백화점
—
camping 캠핑
jazz dance 재즈댄스
climb 오르다
hard 열심히
save 절약하다
—
audition 오디션
since 이래로
Judo 유도
speech contest 말하기 대회
competition (경연) 대회
—
flute 플루트
heavily 심하게
boxing 권투
keep in touch 연락을 유지하다
electric 전자의
—
cable car 케이블카

LESSON 6

release 공개하다
Parents' Day 어버이날
recommend 추천하다
break 깨다
design 디자인하다
—
package 소포
locate 위치하다
tomb 묘
fortress 요새
theater 극장
—
cacao 카카오
ghost 유령
coin 동전
piggy bank 돼지저금통
need 필요
—
indeed 정말로
result 결과
true 사실인
beauty 아름다움
onion 양파
—
pajamas 잠옷
cotton 면
skin 피부
goose down 거위 털
leather 가죽
—
director 감독
direct 감독하다
composition (음악) 작품, 작곡
compose 작곡하다
composer 작곡가
—
piece 조각상
downtown 시내로
amusement park 놀이공원
repair 수리하다
dust 먼지
—
wife 부인
cultural 문화의
icon 상징
tourist 관광객
chain 체인
—
hold 개최하다

ago 전에
parade 퍼레이드
beer 맥주

LESSON 7

favor 청, 부탁
sign 서명하다
turn on (전기 · 가스 · 수도 등을) 켜다
air conditioner 에어컨
turn off (전기 · 가스 · 수도 등을) 끄다
—
recommend 추천하다
slowly 느리게, 천천히
tired 피곤한, 지친
take a break 쉬다, 휴식을 취하다
take an order 주문을 받다
—
hang 걸다, 매달다
hold 붙들다, 잡다
airport 공항
fasten 매다, 채우다
energy 에너지, 동력 자원
—
brush 솔질을 하다
tooth 이, 치아
meal 식사, 끼니
apologize 사과하다
keep a promise 약속을 지키다
—
careful 조심하는, 주의 깊은
school zone 어린이보호구역
motorcycle 오토바이
floor 바닥
slippery 미끄러운
—
within (특정 기간) 이내에
lock 잠그다
check out (호텔 등에서) 나가다, 체크아웃하다
turn down (소리 · 온도 등을) 낮추다
fold 접다
—
allergic 알레르기가 있는
peanut 땅콩
due ~하기로 되어 있는, 예정된
traffic light 신호등
sunscreen 자외선 차단제
—
follow 따르다
lipstick 립스틱
wrap up 싸다, 포장하다
housewarming 집들이
secret 비밀의
—
costume 의상, 복장
exhibition 전시회
rehearse 리허설을 하다

LESSON 8

enough 충분한
exercise 운동하다
surprised 놀란
raise 올리다, 들다
pleased 기쁜
—
receive 받다, 받아들이다
living room 거실
gold medal 금메달
bottle 병
password 비밀번호
—
different 다른
dentist 치과 의사
heat up 따뜻하게 데우다
do the dishes 설거지하다
stationary store 문방구
—
savings account 예금 계좌
package 소포
fence 울타리
through …을 통해
audition 오디션
—
ring 울리다, (초인종을) 누르다
doorbell 초인종
worried 걱정하는
oversleep 늦잠 자다
alarm clock 자명종, 알람 시계
—
ride 타다
view 경관, 전망
amazing (감탄스럽도록) 놀라운
artwork 미술품
pot 냄비, 솥
—
lantern 랜턴, 손전등

LESSON 9

happen 발생하다
shock 충격을 주다, 깜짝 놀라게 하다
fall 떨어지다
fortunately 다행스럽게도, 운 좋게도
bore 지루하게 하다
—
satisfy 만족시키다
result 결과, 결실
boil 삶다
find 찾다, 발견하다
disappoint 실망시키다
—
cheer 환호하다, 응원하다
frighten 겁먹게 만들다
scream 비명을 지르다
catch a cold 감기가 들다
typhoon 태풍
—
clerk 직원, 점원
give up on 포기하다
dessert 후식
text message 문자 메시지
surf 검색하다
—
pumpkin 호박
vampire 흡혈귀
ghost 유령, 귀신
burn 불타다
dangerous 위험한
—
mistake 실수
used 중고의
touch 감동시키다
detective 탐정
thrill 오싹하게 하다
—
sci-fi 공상 과학 소설(의)

LESSON 10

hamster 햄스터
holiday 휴일
popular 인기있는
dish 요리
laptop 노트북
—
battery 배터리
thanks to ~덕분에
bridge 다리
state 주
club 동아리
—
Antarctica 남극
subject 과목
steak 스테이크
rating 평가
price 가격
—
long jumper 멀리뛰기선수
figure skater 피겨스케이트선수
lift (위로) 들어 올리다
weightlifter 역도선수
comfortable 편안한
—
diligent 부지런한
comedian 코미디언
feather 깃털
wool 모직
fashionable 유행하는
—
scarf 스카프
soft 부드러운
silk 실크
convenient 편리한
eat out 외식하다

LESSON 11

recipe 조리법
wrong 틀린
plan 계획
useful 유용한
advice 충고
—
bathroom 화장실
recommend 추천하다
look for 찾다
these days 요즘
borrow 빌리다
—
join 합류하다
topic 주제
grammar 문법
gym shoes 운동화
locker 락커
—
dish 요리

fit 꼭맞다
talent 재능
refrigerator 냉장고
do one's best 최선을 다하다
—
own 자신의
surfing 파도타기
surfboard 서핑보드
language 언어
on sale 할인 중인
—
school song 교가
character 등장인물
unique 독특한
piece 조각
exchange 교환하다

LESSON 12

nail 못
true 진정한
enjoyable 즐거운
index 색인
volunteer work 자원봉사활동
—
make noise 소란을 피우다
gallery 미술관
consider 고려하다
regularly 규칙적으로
take notes 필기하다
—
ahead 앞서
stay up all night 밤새다
during 동안
cheat (시험에서) 부정행위하다
report card 성적표
—
mosquito 모기
perm 파마
refund 환불
bore 지루하게 만들다
do dishes 설거지하다
—
take medicine 약을 복용하다
stain 얼룩지게 하다
jam (기계에 무엇이 끼어) 움직이지 않다
repairman 수리공
vet 수의사
—
treat 치료하다

midterm exam 중간고사
sore throat 인후염
apologize 사과하다
pull out 빼다
—
turn down (소리 등을) 낮추다
burn 타다
remove 제거하다
pimple 여드름
upset 언짢은
—
annoyed 짜증이 난
in front of ~ 앞에
inside ~내부에
stadium 경기장
crowd 군중

지은이

NE능률 영어교육연구소

NE능률 영어교육연구소는 혁신적이며 효율적인 영어 교재를 개발하고
영어 학습의 질을 한 단계 높이고자 노력하는 NE능률의 연구조직입니다.

Writing Builder 2

펴 낸 이 주민홍
펴 낸 곳 서울특별시 마포구 월드컵북로 396(상암동) 누리꿈스퀘어 비즈니스타워 10층
(주)NE능률 (우편번호 03925)
펴 낸 날 2013년 1월 10일 초판 제1쇄 발행
2024년 2월 15일 제18쇄
전 화 02 2014 7114
팩 스 02 3142 0356
홈페이지 www.neungyule.com
등록번호 제 1-68호
ISBN 978-89-6694-539-9 53740
정 가 10,000원

NE 능률

고객센터

교재 내용 문의 : contact.nebooks.co.kr (별도의 가입 절차 없이 작성 가능)
제품 구매, 교환, 불량, 반품 문의 : 02-2014-7114
☎ 전화문의는 본사 업무시간 중에만 가능합니다.

NE능률 교재 MAP

듣기
말하기
쓰기

아래 교재 MAP을 참고하여 본인의 현재 혹은 목표 수준에 따라 교재를 선택하세요.
NE능률 교재들과 함께 영어실력을 쑥쑥~ 올려보세요!
MP3 등 교재 부가 학습 서비스 및 자세한 교재 정보는 www.nebooks.co.kr 에서 확인하세요.

초1-2

초3
- 리스닝버디 1

초3-4
- 리스닝버디 2
- 초등영어 리스닝튜터 Beginner 1
- 초등영어 리스닝튜터 Beginner 2
- 초등영어 리스닝튜터 Beginner 3
- 능률 초등영어 듣기모의고사 10회 4-1, 4-2

초4-5
- 리스닝버디 3
- 능률 초등영어 듣기모의고사 10회 5-1, 5-2

초5-6
- 초등영어 리스닝튜터 Intermediate 1
- 초등영어 리스닝튜터 Intermediate 2
- 초등영어 리스닝튜터 Intermediate 3
- 능률 초등영어 듣기모의고사 10회 6-1, 6-2

초6-예비중
- Writing Builder 1

중1
- 1316 Listening 1
- 능률중학영어 듣기모의고사 22회 1
- Junior Listening Expert 1
- Writing Builder 2
- 쓰기로 마스터하는 중학서술형 1학년

중1-2
- 1316 Listening 2
- 능률중학영어 듣기모의고사 22회 2
- Junior Listening Expert 2

중2-3
- 1316 Listening 3
- Junior Listening Expert 3
- Writing Builder 3
- 쓰기로 마스터하는 중학서술형 2학년

중3
- 능률중학영어 듣기모의고사 22회 3
- Junior Listening Expert 4
- 쓰기로 마스터하는 중학서술형 3학년

중3-예비고

고1
- TEPS BY STEP L+V Basic

고1-2

고2-3
- TEPS BY STEP L+V 1

고3

수능 이상/ 토플 80-89 · 텝스 327-384점
- TEPS BY STEP L+V 2
- RADIX TOEFL Blue Label Listening 1
- RADIX TOEFL Blue Label Listening 2

수능 이상/ 토플 90-99 · 텝스 385-451점
- RADIX TOEFL Black Label Listening 1

수능 이상/ 토플 100 · 텝스 452점 이상
- TEPS BY STEP L+V 3
- RADIX TOEFL Black Label Listening 2

WRITING BUILDER

정답

2

SECTION 1
SENTENCE STRUCTURE

LESSON 1
문장의 형식

UNIT 1
pp. 10~11

A
1 The bread feels very soft.
2 The students kept quiet in the classroom.
3 The weather became warm.
4 Bell invented the telephone in 1876.
5 My mother is a make-up artist.
6 Tim invited me to his party.
7 I got an email this morning.

B
1 Your plan sounds interesting.
2 I lost my cell phone in the library.
3 The woman is a famous professor in Korea.
4 We enjoyed the rock festival yesterday.
5 The potato pizza smells delicious.
6 Our English teacher seems kind.
7 This medicine tastes bitter.
8 Victor prepared dinner for his parents.

C
1 1) I like Kim Yuna very much.
2) She is a famous figure skater.
3) Her performance looks amazing.
2 1) I like Jamie Oliver very much.
2) He is a famous cook.
3) His food tastes delicious.

UNIT 2
pp. 12~13

A
1 Emma made me some pizza.
2 We expected the athlete to win a gold medal.
3 They named their baby Sam.
4 Ron sent me a text message.
5 I found the website useful.
6 Dan wanted me to come to the party.

B
1 I showed my friends my picture.
2 The movie made him a famous director.
3 Ms. Baker taught us English last year.
4 My teacher advised me to read a lot of books.
5 Harry found the exam difficult.
6 Eva lent me her notebook yesterday.
7 My parents told me to come home early.
8 Kevin kept the window open.

C
1 1) sent Jenny flowers
2) It made her happy.
2 1) asked Sarah a difficult question
2) It made her nervous.

WRAP UP
pp. 14~16

A
1 Her father made lunch for her.
2 She ate *tteokbokki* for lunch.
3 It tasted very spicy.
4 She drank a lot of water.

B
1 gave her an alarm clock, He wanted her to get up early.
2 made her a scarf, She wanted her to stay warm.
3 sent her a bicycle, He wanted her to exercise.
4 wrote her cards, They wanted her to be happy.

C
1 His story sounded very sad.
2 Amy bought her mother a nice hat.
3 People call Olivia an angel.
4 The baby's skin feels soft.
5 I showed Tom my new smartphone.
6 The cooler keeps the food fresh.
7 Andy became an English teacher.
8 My mother told me to bring an umbrella today.

D
1 1) It looked very warm.
2) His mother bought him the coat.
2 1) I felt dizzy this morning.
2) The doctor told me to get some rest.

E
1 1) I read a fantasy novel, *Max Hunter*.
2) It was very fun and exciting.
3) I want you to read the novel.
2 1) I watched a war drama, *The Great War*.
2) It was very serious and moving.
3) I want you to watch the drama.

F

1 The potato soup tasted too salty. / She found the potato soup too salty.

2 She told[asked] the waiter to bring another bowl of soup.

LESSON 2
문장 형식의 심화

UNIT 1

pp. 18~19

A

1 My brother made me cook ramen.
2 I heard Joe play the flute.
3 People felt the building shake.
4 Our P.E. teacher had us run fast.
5 We watched the man do magic.
6 I hear the dog bark every night.
7 My teacher let me go home early.
8 I saw Ted cross the street.

B

1 We saw the sun rise over the sea.
2 My mother makes[has] me clean my room.
3 I felt someone touch my bag.
4 My sister doesn't let me wear her clothes.
5 Amy heard her father talk on the phone.
6 My parents made[had] me learn taekwondo.
7 Jim let me read his essay yesterday.

C

1 1) I saw Jungi wear white jeans.
2) They made him look slimmer.

2 1) I saw Misun wear high heels.
2) They made her look taller.

UNIT 2

pp. 20~21

A

1 Emily stayed in England for two weeks.
2 Joe comes to school on time every day.
3 I check the weather with my smartphone every morning.
4 You should come home before sunset.
5 I watched the news on TV yesterday.
6 My father goes to work by bicycle on Fridays.
7 Lucy was at home in the afternoon.
8 Jason met his friends in the park at five.

B

1 I lived in Busan last year.
2 Dan goes to church by bus on Sundays.
3 Sarah read a book in the library for three hours.
4 I took a shower with cold water in the morning.
5 He will arrive at the airport at six thirty.
6 I waited at the bus stop for thirty minutes.
7 Eva works at the restaurant on weekends.
8 He drew the picture with a pencil yesterday.

C

1 1) I will go to Jeju by ship on October 16th.
2) I will stay in Jeju for three days.

2 1) I will go to Gyeongju by KTX on August 3rd.
2) I will stay in Gyeongju for the weekend.

WRAP UP

pp. 22~24

A

1 She heard people scream near the Viking ride.
2 She felt someone touch her shoulder in the haunted house.
3 She watched cartoon characters walk down the street (in a parade).

B

1 Minji[She] goes to the library by subway at 11:20 a.m.
2 Minji[She] goes to the music school by bus at 3:30 p.m.
3 Minji[She] goes home on foot at 5:00 p.m.

C

1 Chris heard someone call his name.
2 Linda studied French in Paris for two years.
3 The coach watched the players pass the ball.
4 Mr. Pitt makes me practice the piano every day.
5 I bought this skirt with my credit card last Sunday.
6 I saw Sarah eat lunch with her friends.
7 David will go to Japan by ship this Saturday.
8 My brother let me use his tablet PC last night.

D

1 1) She saw us fight.
2) She made us clean the classroom.

2 1) I went to Busan by KTX yesterday.
2) We swam in the sea in the afternoon.

E

1 1) I went to Namsan today.
2) I went there on foot.
3) I saw many people ride cable cars.

2 1) I went to Yeouido today.
2) I went there by subway.
3) I saw many people enjoy cherry blossoms.

F

1 two girls draw a line
2 The teacher made a tall boy put out bases.
3 The teacher made a girl bring a ball.

LESSON 3
문장의 확장 I

UNIT 1

pp. 26~27

A

1 Turn off the heater before you go out.
2 When you cross the street, you must be careful.
3 Dohyung wiped the table while his mother was preparing dinner. / While Dohyung wiped the table, his mother was preparing dinner.
4 Before you swim, you should warm up.
5 Cindy lived in Sydney when she was ten years old. / When Cindy lived in Sydney, she was ten years old.
6 While Mike was watching the baseball game, he fell asleep.
7 I can play a computer game after I finish my homework.
8 While I am at my uncle's house, take care of my dog.
9 When I traveled around England, the weather was beautiful.

B

1 Before it rained, we arrived at home.
2 While Tom traveled[was traveling] in Europe, he made many friends.
3 After I graduate, I want to become a writer.
4 When Allie came home, she looked tired.
5 Before you go out, please close the window.

UNIT 2

pp. 27~28

A

1 Peter went to bed early because he felt sick.
2 If you are hungry, you can eat lunch now.
3 There was a traffic jam, so I took the subway.
4 Unless you study hard, you won't get good grades.
5 Because it was too hot, I couldn't sleep well.
6 I will go to the amusement park if it is sunny tomorrow.

B

1 I was too cold, so I turned on the heater.
2 Because Jay was sick, he didn't attend the meeting.
3 If you see Harry, tell him to come to the party.
4 Because I got up late, I didn't have breakfast.
5 Unless you wear[If you don't wear] a warm coat, you will catch a cold.

UNIT 3

pp. 28~29

A

1 Many students think that math is difficult.
2 I know that my parents love me very much.
3 Dan said that he lost his wallet last week.
4 Let's imagine that we are on the moon.
5 We believe that our team will win first prize.
6 I think that Jessica is the smartest in our class.
7 Jim hopes that he will travel to China this summer.

B

1 1) I think that my mother shops online too much.
2) I hope that she shops[will shop] online less.
2 1) I think that my brother plays games too much.
2) I hope that he plays[will play] games less.

WRAP UP

pp. 30~32

A

1 Make a study plan before you study.
2 Review the class materials after the class finishes.
3 Take notes when you are in class.

B

1 I think that traveling gives us a good rest.
2 I think that the Internet gives us useful information.
3 I think that friends give us a lot of enjoyment.

C

1 When Indians eat, they use their hands.
2 I lost my cell phone, so I couldn't call you.
3 Because the hat was too expensive, Joan didn't buy it.
4 After the train left, I arrived at the station.
5 Unless you have[If you don't have] a library card,

you can't borrow books.
6 While Ron was waiting, he read a magazine.
7 I believe that David will become a good soccer player.

D

1 1) Katie didn't come to school today because she was sick. / Because Katie was sick, she didn't come to school today.
2) When I called her, she was sleeping. / She was sleeping when I called her.
2 1) I will go to the department store after school is over. / After school is over, I will go to the department store.
2) I hope that they (will) like my presents.

E

1 1) I think that the design is pretty.
2) But they seem tight when I wear them.
2 1) I think that the size is small.
2) But it seems heavy when I carry it.

F

1 Online classes are good because students can save money.
I think that they are useful.
[추가 답안] Online classes are good because students can take classes again later.
I think that they are helpful.
2 Online classes are bad because students can skip class easily.
I think that they are not useful.
[추가 답안] Online classes are bad because students can't focus on classes.
I think that they are not helpful.

LESSON 4
문장의 확장 II

UNIT 1

pp. 34~35

A

1 Taemin has some friends who want to be singers.
2 Steve has a cat which has black fur.
3 The man who is a hairdresser lives next door.
4 Julie wants to buy the pants which have big pockets.
5 Pass me the remote control which is on the sofa.
6 The restaurant which opened last Friday was good.
7 Ben is the boy who won first prize.
8 I bought a monitor which has a big screen.
9 The thief who stole money ran away.

B

1 Susie knows the student who is from Spain.
2 Eric has a blog which has a lot of pictures.
3 Marie is a baker who makes delicious cakes.
4 My boyfriend bought me roses which smell sweet.
5 The girl who is wearing a blue hat is my best friend.
6 A strawberry is a fruit which has a lot of vitamin C.
7 Harry is the boy who plays basketball very well.

C

1 1) She is the writer who wrote the *Harry Potter* series.
2) She is a woman who gives people joy.
2 1) He is the singer who donates money to poor people.
2) He is a man who gives people pleasure.

UNIT 2

pp. 36~37

A

1 My teacher liked the essay which Peter wrote.
2 Jason Mraz is the singer whom I wanted to see.
3 This is the talk show which Kevin watches on Fridays.
4 This is the boy whom Jiyeon talked about yesterday.
5 Potato pizza is the food which Sue likes the most.
6 Tell me about the story which you heard today.
7 The man whom I saw on the street was my math teacher.
8 The laptop which my brother bought last week doesn't work.
9 The doctor whom I saw yesterday was very kind to me.

B

1 I didn't receive the books which I ordered last week.
2 Emily remembers the people who(m) she met in Brazil.
3 Julie has the pictures which we took last Saturday.
4 The people who(m) I traveled with were kind.
5 The cookies which Sam baked were really

delicious.

6 Ms. Song is a teacher who(m) we respect.
7 This is the key which Jenny was looking for.
8 *The Simpsons* is the cartoon show which I like the most.

C

1 1) The place which I recommend is Yongin.
2) Yongin has a traditional area which many people visit.
2 1) The place which I recommend is Gyeongju.
2) Gyeongju has a temple which many people visit.

WRAP **UP**

pp. 38~40

A

1 is a person who makes coffee in a coffee shop
2 is a person who takes care of the artwork in a museum
3 is a person who finds errors in new games

B

1 1) Soccer is the sport which Alice likes the most.
2) The team which she supports is Manchester United.
2 1) Basketball is the sport which Harry likes the most.
2) The team which he supports is the LA Lakers.

C

1 Jake is looking for someone who can help him.
2 This is the bag which my mother wants to have.
3 Jim is a friend who(m) I can trust.
4 I lost the watch which my father gave me.
5 The man who is wearing sunglasses is a famous actor.
6 The train which goes to Seoul leaves at 2:00.
7 The wallet which I lost this morning was blue.

D

1 1) I visited my uncle who lives in Orlando.
2) I saw Disney characters which I like.
2 1) We are looking for a girl who sings (songs) very well.
2) visit our practice room which is in the Student Union Building

E

1 1) is next to the movie theater
2) which tastes very fresh
2 1) I recommend Dragon which is in front of the NE school.
2) They sell *tteokbokki* which tastes very spicy.

F

1 who is kicking a ball
2 who is wearing a blue T-shirt
3 who is listening to music

SECTION 2
GRAMMAR FOR WRITING

LESSON 5
시제

UNIT 1

pp. 44~45

A

1 The weather will be fine this weekend.
2 Joe is going to visit his uncle tomorrow.
3 I will lend you my laptop.
4 We are going to arrive on time.
5 I will memorize fifty English words every day.
6 The singer is going to have a concert next month.
7 There will be a big sale at the department store soon.

B

1 is going to take an online class this weekend
2 is going to learn jazz dance this weekend
3 is going to climb Mt. Dobong this weekend

C

1 1) I am going to buy a jacket next month.
2) I will save money for it.
2 1) I am going to take a trip to Egypt this summer.
2) I will make a plan for it.
3 1) I am going to have a dance audition next week.
2) I will practice hard for it.

UNIT 2

pp. 46~47

A

1 I have never eaten pizza at this restaurant before.
2 Linda has liked to sing since she was young.
3 Inho has slept for ten hours.
4 We have played this game once.
5 Julia and Soobin have been friends for three years.
6 Kelly has been to Minji's house several times.
7 Jinsu has learned Judo for six months.

B

1 I have read the *Twilight* series twice.
2 June has been sick since yesterday.
3 I have seen kangaroos in Australia.
4 Sophie has worn glasses since she was eight.
5 Maria has never played golf.
6 Tony has studied Chinese for two years.
7 I have been to Jejudo three times.

C

1 1) has swum for two years
2) She has won a prize at the swimming competition twice.
2 1) has done ballet for seven years
2) He has won a prize at the ballet contest three times.

WRAP UP

pp. 48~50

A

1 to take a trip to Italy
2 have never been to Italy
3 I am going to leave on July 15th.
4 I have prepared for the trip for a month.
5 I am going to go to the Colosseum in Rome.

B

1 He has never learned to play the flute.
2 She has studied Chinese since she was nine.
3 He has learned taekwondo for seven years.

C

1 I will read twelve books this year.
2 It will[is going to] rain heavily this weekend.
3 Jessica has seen[watched] the movie ten times.
4 I have used this cell phone for three years.
5 We will[are going to] arrive thirty minutes late.
6 I am going to take boxing lessons next month.
7 My family has been to Disneyland once.

D

1 1) I am going to move this weekend.
2) I will remember you forever
2 1) I have been to Paris twice.
2) I have liked art since then.

E

1 1) He has played the drums for three years.
2) He has played the drums in our band since 2011.
2 1) She has played the guitar for five years.
2) She has played the electric guitar in our band since 2010.

F

1 1) I have been to Qatar.
2) I have seen[watched] a camel race.
2 1) I have been to Switzerland.
2) I have ridden an open cable car.

LESSON 6
수동태

UNIT 1

pp. 52~53

A

1 The thief was caught by the police officer.
2 The new movie will be released (by them) next Friday.
3 Coca-Cola is drunk by many people all over the world.
4 This 3D TV was made by a Korean company.
5 Dinner will be cooked by me on Parents' Day.
6 The *Harry Potter* series are[were] read by many people.
7 These pictures of babies were taken by Peter.
8 This restaurant was recommended by my friends.

B

1 The singer is loved by many fans.
2 These cookies were baked by Jessica.
3 The mirror was broken by Jason yesterday.
4 Smartphones are used by many people.
5 This dress was designed by a famous designer.
6 The package will be delivered soon.
7 My purse was stolen on the subway yesterday.
8 This book is read by many children.

C

1 1) The Great Wall is located in China.
2) It was built in the 7th century B.C.

3) It was used as a fortress.
2 1) The Colosseum is located in Italy.
2) It was built in 80 A.D.
3) It was used as a theater.

UNIT 2

pp. 54~55

A

1 The floor is covered with a brown carpet.
2 It is said that the movie is boring.
3 This red piggy bank is filled with coins.
4 It is said that a friend in need is a friend indeed.
5 My sister is interested in figure skating.
6 People were surprised at the result of the game.
7 It is said that the story is true.

B

1 The cake was covered with strawberries.
2 All the news is concerned with the Olympic games.
3 My mother was satisfied with their service.
4 It is said that Mr. Johnson is very rich.
5 Jane was surprised at the beauty of Bali.
6 It is said that the mountain is dangerous.
7 My father is interested in playing golf.
8 This soup is made of onions and carrots.

C

1 1) This coat is made of goose down.
2) It is said that goose down keeps us warm.
2 1) These shoes are made of lambskin.
2) It is said that lambskin is softer than leather.

WRAP UP

pp. 56~58

A

1 *Twilight* was written by Stephenie Meyer.
2 The *Mona Lisa* was painted by Leonardo da Vinci.
3 *Wedding March* was composed by Richard Wagner.
4 *The Thinker* was made by Auguste Rodin.

B

1 She was interested in the pink shoes.
2 the shoes were made of leather
3 She was surprised at the price.

C

1 Our classroom is cleaned every day.
2 The amusement park was filled with many people.
3 The computer was repaired by my brother.
4 The books were covered with dust.
5 This money will be used for sick people.
6 It is said that an Indian king built the Taj Mahal for his wife.
7 Ron was satisfied with the test result.

D

1 1) The tower was built in 1889.
2) It was designed by Gustave Eiffel.
2 1) My father and I are interested in climbing a mountain.
2) It is said that Mt. Jili is covered with snow now.

E

1 1) is held
2) was started about 290 years ago
3) is said that
2 1) Oktoberfest is held in Germany.
2) It was started about 200 years ago.
3) It is said that the many kinds of beer are amazing.

F

1 is covered with books
2 is filled with (soccer) balls
3 is made of wood

LESSON 7
조동사

UNIT 1

pp. 60~61

A

1 Would you pass me the book?
2 Could you be quiet?
3 Would you sign here?
4 Could you help me with my homework?
5 Would you tell me your name?
6 Could you show me your ID?
7 Would you give me some water?
8 Could you bring your camera?
9 you could turn on the air conditioner

B

1 Could[Would] you lend me your pen?
2 Could[Would] you close the door?
3 Could[Would] you turn off your cell phone?
4 Could[Would] you recommend a book?
5 Could[Would] you fix my bike[bicycle]?
6 Could[Would] you speak slowly?

7 If you are tired, you could take a break. / You could take a break if you are tired.

C

1 1) Could you hang this picture
2) would you hold this chair

2 1) Could you drive to the airport?
2) Sure, would you fasten your seat belt?

UNIT 2

pp. 62~63

A

1 I have to finish my report.
2 Tom has to apologize to me first.
3 My father had to work late last night.
4 We have to keep our promises.
5 Soobin has to go to the dentist.
6 Henry had to get up early this morning.
7 You have to be careful with the knife.
8 Laura has to help her grandmother this weekend.
9 Yuna had to change trains at City Hall station.

B

1 you must wear a helmet
2 you must turn off your cell phone
3 you must walk carefully

C

1 1) You must come back by 10:00 p.m.
2) You must lock your door

2 1) You must check out by 11:00 a.m.
2) You must return your hotel key

WRAP UP

pp. 64~66

A

1 Could you speak (more) quietly?
2 Could you fold your newspaper?
3 Could you turn down the volume?

B

1 You must return these books (today).
2 You must not cross the street.
3 You must wear sunscreen.
4 You must not take pictures.

C

1 Could[Would] you give me more rice?
2 We must[have to] follow the school rules.
3 Could[Would] you watch my bag?
4 I had to send Katie an email yesterday.
5 Could[Would] you bring me a menu?
6 John must[has to] go to school this Saturday.
7 You could borrow my umbrella.

D

1 1) Could[Would] you recommend a gift for my mother?
2) Could[Would] you wrap up the present?

2 1) I had to do my homework last night.
2) I must[have to] clean the classroom this afternoon

E

1 1) Could you come to the birthday party?
2) You must keep it secret because it is a surprise party.

2 1) Could you come to the Halloween party?
2) You must wear interesting clothes because it is a costume party.

F

1 1) I am sorry, but I must go home.
2) I have to go to my piano lesson.

2 1) I am sorry, but I must go to the science exhibition.
2) I have to do science homework.

LESSON 8
to부정사와 동명사

UNIT 1

pp. 68~69

A

1 We ordered something to eat.
2 My family needs a big sofa to sit on.
3 This is an easy question to solve.
4 They don't have a house to live in.
5 I have something to tell you.
6 She bought a dress to wear at the party.
7 John doesn't have anyone to talk with.
8 Mike needs a box to put toys in.

B

1 Brian bought a comic book to read on the train.
2 Ruby lent me a pen to write with.
3 I am looking for a gift[present] to give my girlfriend.
4 Max needs enough time to exercise.
5 The boys wanted a ball to play with.

UNIT 2

pp. 69~70

A

1 I took a taxi to arrive on time.
2 John was surprised to meet Tom.
3 I raised my hand to ask a question.
4 Max went to the store to buy milk.
5 She was pleased to receive the present.

B

1 Mary cleaned the living room to help her mother.
2 Usain was happy to win a gold medal.
3 Jerry bought some bread to make a sandwich.
4 My sister studied hard to pass the exam.
5 I was angry to see the rude people.
6 We kept the party secret to surprise him.

UNIT 3

pp. 70~71

A

1 I remember seeing Ben in New York.
2 He tried to change his bad habits.
3 Lisa forgot putting the key on the table.
4 Kelly remembered to meet Eva.
5 I tried using a different password to open the door.
6 Emily remembered to go to the dentist.
7 She forgot to return the books today.
8 Andy tried to memorize their names.

B

1 1) Remember to heat up the pizza
2) Don't forget to do the dishes
2 1) Remember to turn off the light
2) Don't forget to lock the door

WRAP UP

pp. 72~74

A

1 Hyunji[She] needs a savings account to put money in. She will go to the bank to open one.
2 Hyunji[She] has a package to send. She will go to the post office to send it.
3 Hyunji[She] needs some milk to drink. She will go to the supermarket to buy some.

B

1 He tried getting[to get] into the house through the window.
2 I remember locking the door.
3 I forgot to close the window.

C

1 I bought something to eat at the convenience store.
2 Susie forgot putting her cell phone in her bag.
3 Jack forgot to bring his math textbook.
4 Ron was happy to pass the audition.
5 Remember to call me at the airport.
6 They did their best to win the game.
7 Paul tried opening the bottle.

D

1 1) she didn't go to school to get some rest
2) She was surprised to see him.
2 1) I forgot to set the alarm
2) I tried to get to school on time

E

1 1) You should go to China to see the Great Wall.
2) There are a lot of great views to enjoy.
3) Remember to watch the amazing circus!
2 1) You should go to France to visit the art museums.
2) There is a lot of great artwork to see.
3) Remember to take a boat ride on the River Seine!

F

1 1) Remember to bring a pot.
2) You will need a pot to cook in.
2 1) Remember to bring a lantern.
2) You will need a lantern to go out at night.

LESSON 9
수식어

UNIT 1

pp. 76~77

A

1 The sleeping baby looks like an angel.
2 Sumi was tired from a long hike.
3 We listened to the sound of the falling rain.
4 My team was satisfied with the result of the game.
5 Don't touch the broken glass.
6 It is exciting to make new friends.

B

1 We ate boiled eggs on the train.
2 John's test grade was disappointing.
3 My father fixed the broken chair.
4 The food at this restaurant is satisfying.
5 I found my lost watch under the bed.
6 People were surprised at the news.

7 Our teacher told us an interesting story during class.

C

1 1) The baseball game was exciting.
2) The excited fans cheered for the team.

2 1) The horror movie was frightening.
2) The frightened people screamed.

UNIT 2

pp. 78~79

A

1 James often catches a cold in winter.
2 Tiffany is usually at home on the weekend.
3 My smartphone sometimes stops working.
4 You must always remember my advice.
5 It is sometimes difficult to make a decision.
6 He usually goes to school by subway.
7 I will never forget the trip to India.
8 Jinsu sometimes visits Tom's blog to see his pictures.
9 Typhoons often came to Jeju this year.

B

1 Jerry sometimes sends me an email.
2 The clerk is always kind to his customers.
3 Susie will never give up on her dream.
4 Katie often buys clothes online.
5 Jenny is usually busy on Mondays.
6 Ron sometimes eats dessert after a meal.
7 You should always keep quiet in the library.

C

1 1) usually uses his tablet PC to watch movies
2) He sometimes reads e-books on it.

2 1) usually uses her smartphone to send text messages
2) She sometimes surfs the Internet on it.

WRAP UP

pp. 80~82

A

1 The laughing boy is wearing a vampire costume.
2 The crying girl is wearing a pumpkin costume.
3 The dancing girl is wearing a princess costume.

B

1 He always walks to school.
2 He never eats fast food.
3 He sometimes plays tennis.
4 He usually goes to bed early.

C

1 The burning building looked very dangerous.
2 Amy sometimes makes mistakes on exams.
3 My uncle bought a used car last year.
4 I will never play computer games from now on.
5 Matt is interested in making films.
6 Julie often eats lunch with Bob.
7 My grades were very satisfying.

D

1 1) I gave him an interesting novel.
2) He looked very touched.

2 1) My family often goes to the restaurant.
2) It will never disappoint you.

E

1 1) The detective story was very thrilling.
2) I was thrilled by the scary story.

2 1) The sci-fi story was very boring.
2) I was bored with the simple story.

F

1 I usually play basketball after school.
2 I sometimes have a basketball game on Sunday morning.
3 I always win the game, and it is (very) interesting.

LESSON 10
비교

UNIT 1

pp. 84~85

A

1 This hamster is as small as my hand.
2 August is the hottest month of the year.
3 This play is more exciting than the book.
4 Sumin's room is as big as her sister's.
5 Drinking juice is better than drinking Coke.
6 Chuseok is one of the biggest holidays in Korea.

B

1 Jane's computer is as old as yours.
2 An orange is sweeter than a lemon.
3 I bought the cheapest cell phone in the store[shop].
4 Basketball is as popular as baseball in the USA.
5 I like singing more than dancing.
6 Pizza is one of the most popular dishes in the world.

C

1 1) The Ocean laptop is smaller than the Air laptop.

2) The Ocean laptop's battery life is the shortest of the three.

2 1) The Air laptop is as heavy as the Ocean laptop.

2) The Air laptop is the largest[biggest] of the three.

UNIT 2

pp. 86~87

A

1 Alaska is bigger than any other state in the USA.
2 No animal is smarter than man.
3 No player in our club is as young as Amanda.
4 Joe is taller than any other student in his class.
5 No place in the world is colder than Antarctica.
6 No singer in China is as popular as her.
7 Carlos is richer than any other man in his country.

B

1 No country in the world is bigger[larger] than Russia.
2 No subject is as interesting as history.
3 Kiwis have more vitamin C than any other fruit.
4 No girl in our class is faster than Maria.
5 No building in this city is as old as this school.
6 This is lighter than any other coat in this store[shop].
7 No dish in this restaurant is as expensive as steak.
8 No material in the world is harder than diamonds.

C

1 1) Mt. Baekdu is taller than any other mountain in Korea.

2) No mountain in the world is taller than Mt. Everest.

2 1) The Nakdong River is longer than any other river in Korea.

2) No river in the world is longer than the Nile River.

WRAP UP

pp. 88~90

A

1 is as cheap[expensive] as
2 has better service than
3 is as old[new] as
4 is more expensive than
5 has the worst service of

B

1 No long jumper in the world jumped as far as Mike.
2 No figure skater in the world was better than Yuna.
3 No runner in the world ran as fast as Usain.
4 Miran lifted a heavier weight than any other weightlifter in the world.

C

1 No place is as comfortable as my house.
2 Michael Jackson was one of the best singers in the world.
3 The movie was more interesting than the book.
4 Max is the youngest of the three brothers.
5 No player on our team is as good as Jordan.
6 John is more diligent than any other student in my class.
7 No flower is more beautiful than man.

D

1 1) Steve is the most popular boy in our class.

2) he is as funny as a comedian

2 1) She was more beautiful than a flower.

2) No girl in the world is prettier than her.

E

1 1) You will feel that these gloves are as warm as wool.

2) No gloves are more fashionable than these!

2 1) You will feel that this scarf is as soft as a silk.

2) No scarf is more beautiful than this!

F

1 Eating out is usually more convenient than eating at home.
[추가 답안] Eating out is usually quicker than eating at home.

2 Eating out is usually more expensive than eating at home.
[추가 답안] Eating out is usually more unhealthy than eating at home.

LESSON 11
대명사

UNIT 1

pp. 92~93

A

1 My teacher gave me some useful advice.
2 There is not any toilet paper in the bathroom.

3 These oranges are too small, so I want bigger ones.
4 I looked for my key, but I couldn't find it.
5 Are there any interesting movies these days?
6 Would you like some more chocolate cake?
7 I forgot to bring my pens, but I could borrow one.

B

1 Sue watched some movies at home last Sunday.
2 My computer is too old, so I want to buy a new one.
3 Some of my friends joined a soccer club.
4 Do you have any questions about the topic?
5 Would you like (to have) some doughnuts?
6 Karen likes listening to old songs more than new ones.
7 Maria didn't have any homework yesterday.

C

1 1) But he doesn't have any sketchbooks.
2) He wants to buy one.
2 1) But she doesn't have any gym shoes.
2) She wants to buy ones[some].

UNIT 2

pp. 94~95

A

1 Every student in this school has a locker.
2 All the people in my family get together on New Year's Day.
3 Each person orders a different dish.
4 No clothes in this store fit me.

B

1 Every student in our class likes our math teacher. / All (of) the students in our class like our math teacher.
2 Each person has a different talent.
3 Patrick got an A in all (of) the subjects. / Partick got an A in every subject.
4 Both (of) my American friends like Korean food.
5 There is no milk in the refrigerator.
6 All (of) the players did their best at the game. / Every player did their best at the game.
7 Each of us has our own hobby.

C

1 1) go wind-surfing every summer
2) Both like wind-surfing a lot.
3) Each of them has a surfboard.
2 1) go mountain biking every fall
2) Both like mountain biking a lot.
3) Each of them has a mountain bike.

WRAP UP

pp. 96~98

A

1 Both (of them) are soccer players.
2 She doesn't have any money.
3 Each person[of them] speaks a different language.

B

1 Each teddy bear[of the teddy bears] in the store has a price tag.
2 Some (of the) teddy bears in the store are on sale.
3 No teddy bears in the store are wearing shoes.

C

1 Jessica solved all (of) the problems[every problem] on time.
2 Sara doesn't have any classes on Saturday. / Sara has no classes on Saturday.
3 Each school[of the schools] has its own school song.
4 Mike sold his old camera, and he bought a new one.
5 Both of us ordered steak for lunch.
6 Every dish in this restaurant is delicious. / All (of) the dishes in this restaurant are delicious.
7 James bought some bread at the bakery.

D

1 1) All (of) the T-shirts were 30%~50% off. / Every T-shirt was 30%~50% off.
2) she couldn't find any nice T-shirts
2 1) Each movie has a different story.
2) Every character is unique and interesting. / All (of) the characters are unique and interesting.

E

1 1) Every item is on sale.
2) We provide 30 percent off on each item.
2 1) Every member uses a locker for free.
2) We provide a personal trainer for each member.

F

1 ordered some shirts
2 All (of) the shirts[All of them] were big for me.
3 I asked to exchange them for smaller ones.

LESSON 12
자주 쓰이는 표현

UNIT 1

pp. 100~101

A

1 Mary thinks it enjoyable to play tennis.
2 I found it fun to spend time at the mall.
3 Jessica felt it wrong to fight with friends.
4 The index made it easy to find the words.
5 Max considers it important to do volunteer work.
6 We found it difficult to write an email in English.
7 People think it rude to make noise in a gallery.

B

1 Eddie thinks it important to wear a helmet.
2 Jessi found it interesting[fun] to learn Korean.
3 Nancy felt it necessary to help poor children.
4 The signs make it easy to find the restaurant.
5 People consider it important to exercise regularly.
6 Ron thinks it wrong to break the rules.
7 I found it impossible to arrive on time.

C

1 1) I found it important to take notes.
2) I found it wrong to sleep during class.
2 1) I found it important to read the questions carefully.
2) I found it wrong to cheat on exam.

UNIT 2

pp.102~103

A

1 Lily got a refund for the shirt.
2 Serena got her nails painted yesterday.
3 Karen got bored with the work.
4 After I watched the movie, I got sad.
5 Julie often gets invited to the birthday parties.
6 My father gets our dog to bring the newspaper.
7 We can[are able to] get a lot of information on the Internet.
8 Henry's girlfriend got him to start exercising.

B

1 It gets dark at 6:00 p.m. these days.
2 Joe got a Christmas card from his grandparents.
3 My cat got hit by a bicycle yesterday.
4 Tom got his father's car washed.
5 Mary got her sister to do dishes.
6 If you take this medicine, you will get better soon. / You will get better soon if you take this medicine.
7 We got our homework finished on time.

C

1 1) My printer got jammed.
2) So I got the repairman to fix it.
2 1) My dog got hurt.
2) So I got the vet to treat it.

WRAP UP

pp. 104~106

A

1 She thought it wise to wear a scarf.
2 She thought it wise to visit an eye doctor.
3 He thought it wise to buy a new one.
4 She thought it wise to apologize first.

B

1 She got her tooth pulled out.
2 She got her computer repaired.
3 She got a pizza delivered.

C

1 I got my brother to carry my bags.
2 Eva found it difficult to keep pets.
3 The man got his car repaired.
4 Sue got many presents on her birthday.
5 I thought it right to tell the truth.
6 Ted got his brother to turn down the volume.
7 Some students feel it better to study in the morning.

D

1 1) My skin got burned badly.
2) I found it necessary to use sunscreen.
2 1) Our English teacher got us to practice the play every day.
2) we got better

E

1 1) They said that this drink makes it easy to lose weight.
2) But I got fatter because of it, and I got angry.
2 1) They said that this spray makes it easy to wash windows.
2) But my window got dirtier because of it, and I got annoyed.

F

1 You will find it fun[exciting] to cheer with other fans.
[추가 답안] You will find it exciting[fun] to watch

the game right in front of you.

2 You will find it expensive to buy snacks inside the stadium.
[추가 답안] You will find it annoying to walk through the crowds.

SECTION 3
PATTERNS FOR WRITING

Useful Patterns for Writing 1

1 The kids were curious about the small animal.
2 Rosa was aware of her problem.
3 I am curious about stars in the sky.
4 David is aware of my bad habits.
5 He was curious about our new plan.
6 We are aware of our situation.
7 People are curious about his new book.
8 Jane is aware of the important fact.
9 Sally was curious about the handsome actor.
10 They are aware of the school rules.

Useful Patterns for Writing 2

1 I disagree[don't agree] with my sister.
2 I am against your plan.
3 I agreed with Sam's suggestion.
4 They are against the rules.
5 Tom will agree with his wife.
6 We are against this war.
7 She disagreed[didn't agree] with my decision.
8 Amy was against the solution.
9 Susan agreed with John's argument.
10 We are against the new policy.

Useful Patterns for Writing 3

1 I don't think that Lily is kind.
2 I suggest that you (should) watch this action movie.
3 I don't think that this watch is cheap.
4 Doctors recommend that we (should) drink a lot of water.
5 I don't think that it will rain tomorrow.
6 He suggested that we (should) leave home early.
7 I don't think that Emma is a good singer.
8 She recommended that I (should) visit the museum.
9 I don't think that money is very important.
10 Jenny suggested that we (should) travel to Jejudo.

Useful Patterns for Writing 4

1 Sally seems[appears] to like you.
2 I am worried about my test results.
3 He seemed[appeared] to be very tired.
4 Nick is worried about his daughter's health.
5 You seem[appear] to have many friends.
6 I am worried about his unhealthy diet.
7 She seemed[appeared] to enjoy swimming.
8 Julie was worried about her presentation.
9 He seems[appears] to believe my story.
10 My parents are worried about my future.

Useful Patterns for Writing 5

1 She nearly forgot that she had a meeting.
2 I will never forget your help.
3 Ava completely forgot about her promise.
4 He never forgot his country.
5 He nearly forgot about his uncle's wedding.
6 I will never forget my middle school friends.
7 We completely forgot that he was waiting for us.
8 She never forgot David's soft voice.
9 I nearly forgot about my English homework.
10 I will never forget the last scene.

Useful Patterns for Writing 6

1 You are allowed to check out four books.
2 She is likely to arrive late.
3 Students were allowed to go home early today.
4 Jack is likely to pass the exam.
5 We were allowed to watch TV for an hour.
6 They are likely to stay at[in] this hotel.
7 Visitors were allowed to enter this building.
8 Emily is likely to cancel the plan.
9 They are allowed to play basketball here.
10 Rick is likely to join a tennis club.

Useful Patterns for Writing 7

1 I would like to go shopping.
2 Would you mind going with me?
3 I would like to wash my face.

4 Would you mind closing this window?
5 I would like to eat a hamburger.
6 Would you mind lending me your bicycle?
7 I would like to visit your office tomorrow.
8 Would you mind taking my picture?
9 I would like to be[become] a science teacher.
10 Would you mind lowering the volume?

Useful Patterns for Writing 8

1 Remember to turn off the computer in the classroom.
2 Don't forget to clean the bathroom.
3 Remember borrowing some money from me.
4 Don't forget to ask Amy her phone number.
5 Remember to take your umbrella.
6 Don't forget to invite your friends.
7 Remember working together for the project.
8 Don't forget to send us your photos.
9 Remember to return this book tomorrow.
10 Don't forget to lock the door.

Useful Patterns for Writing 9

1 I am interested in making bags.
2 I don't have any interest in playing computer games.
3 She is not interested in studying science.
4 Justin doesn't have much interest in sports.
5 We are interested in French food.
6 I don't have any interest in golf.
7 Grace is not interested in marriage.
8 We don't have much interest in history.
9 Sean is interested in buying a house.
10 Amanda doesn't have any interest in cars.

Useful Patterns for Writing 10

1 He thinks my car is better than yours.
2 I sent the letters as early as I could.
3 My mother thinks drinking milk is better than drinking water.
4 Alex walked as fast as he could.
5 He thinks swimming is better than running.
6 I will call you back as soon as I can.
7 People think her second album is better than the first one.
8 Lucy is working as hard as she can.
9 I think experiencing is better than reading books.
10 Sam spoke as loud as he could.

Useful Patterns for Writing 11

1 All you have to do is sign here.
2 The more he has, the more he wants.
3 All you have to do is study harder.
4 The older I get, the more tired I feel.
5 All you have to do is be quiet.
6 The longer Andrew stayed in India, the more he liked the country.
7 All you have to do is win this game.
8 The more you do this exercise, the healthier you will become.
9 All you have to do is close your eyes.
10 The higher I went up, the colder the air got[became].

Useful Patterns for Writing 12

1 You are not supposed to open this box.
2 Patrick looks forward to working with you.
3 We are supposed to paint our house today.
4 We are looking forward to watching her new movie.
5 I was supposed to leave last week.
6 I look forward to making new friends here.
7 We are not supposed to smoke in this building.
8 Mary is looking forward to talking with you again.
9 You are not supposed to park here.
10 We are looking forward to going camping next week.